The Cat's Pyjamas

McDonald's Young Writers

A collection of writings, winners in a competition for young writers organised by McDonald's and The O'Brien Press.

Work was submitted from all parts of Ireland, in both Irish and English languages. Included were short stories, poems, plays, journalistic pieces - the fanciful, the realistic, the sensitive and socially aware. These works reflect a broad range of interests among young writers.

'excellent by any standards, and shows that Ireland will never be short of writing talent'
BOOKS IRELAND

THESE WINNING ENTRIES TO THE McDONALD'S YOUNG WRITERS COMPETITION WERE SELECTED BY AN INDEPENDENT PANEL OF EXPERT JUDGES OF CHILDREN'S WRITING. CHAIRPERSON OF THE PANEL WAS DR. PAT DONLON, DIRECTOR OF THE NATIONAL LIBRARY OF IRELAND, AND THE JURORS WERE: MARY FINN, CHILDREN'S EDITOR OF THE RTE GUIDE, DR. TINA HICKEY, LINGUISTICS INSTITUTE OF IRELAND, TOM McCAUGHREN, WELL-KNOWN AUTHOR OF CHILDREN'S FICTION, AND FINIAN O'SHEA, A TEACHER.

ROYALTIES FROM THE SALE OF *THE CAT'S PYJAMAS* WILL GO TO THE IRISH CHILDREN'S BOOK TRUST.

The Cat's Pyjamas

McDonald's Young Writers

THE PRIZEWINNING
COLLECTION

Illustrations by
DONALD TESKEY

THE O'BRIEN PRESS
DUBLIN

First published 1992 by The O'Brien Press Ltd.,
20 Victoria Road, Dublin 6, Ireland.

Copyright © McDonald's Corporation
and The O'Brien Press Ltd. 1992

All rights reserved. No part of this book may be reproduced or utilised in any form or by any means, electronic or mechanical, including photocopying, recording or by any information storage and retrieval system without permission in writing from the publisher. This book may not be sold as a bargain book or at a reduced price without permission in writing from the publisher.

10 9 8 7 6 5 4 3 2

British Library Cataloguing in Publication Data
Cat's Pyjamas: McDonald's Young Writers -
The Prize-winning Collection
I. Teskey, Donald
823.008 [J]
ISBN 0-86278-289-9

Typesetting, layout and design: The O'Brien Press
Cover separations: The City Office, Dublin
Printing: The Guernsey Press, Guernsey, Channel Islands

All applicants have been asked to verify that their entry is an original work. The publishers accept no responsibility if this requirement has not been fulfilled.

FOREWORD

It has been said that to suppress creativity is to deny achievement, and nowhere is this more relevant than in the case of children. As young people develop, so too does their imagination and ability to express themselves in their own unique ways, most particularly through the medium of writing.

McDonald's have recognised the wealth of talent that exists amongst Ireland's young writers and has established the McDonald's Young Writers Competition with the aim of encouraging and promoting the enjoyment of creative writing.

The Cat's Pyjamas reflects the variety of thoughts coming through the minds of Ireland's young people. It is therefore most appropriate that royalties from sales of the book will benefit the Irish Children's Book Trust.

To all who have guided this book from inception to final production, I offer the heartfelt thanks of the Irish licensees of McDonald's. Particular credit is due to Dr. Pat Donlon, Chairperson, and to all the members of the selection jury for their concerted effort in selecting stories, the results of which you now see before you.

Michael G. Mehigan
Chairman of McDonald's Licensee Group in Ireland

A WORD FROM THE JURY

When the judges agreed to serve on the panel for the McDonald's Young Writers Project, they could not have imagined that on this island everywhere pens were poised, pencils sharpened and even in some instances word processors switched to 'on'. The sheer volume of entries was staggering, as indeed one imagines were the postmen who carried the entries from all over the country.

The budding authors wrote poems, plays, prose pieces and short stories on a great variety of topics. Topics ranged from the destruction of the rainforests, oil and the 'troubles' to raindrops and rainbows, families and fairytales. The overall standard of entries was high, making the task of the judges almost impossible. Pieces were selected for the imaginative qualities, their originality, style and ability to describe the ordinary and everyday as well as depict the futuristic and the fantastic. The jury was particularly impressed with the Irish language entries. These pieces show a confidence and clarity of style together with a delight in language which is worthy of comment and commendation.

Parents and teachers too deserve a word of praise for encouraging and endorsing the young writers' endeavours. But all the glittering prizes go to the writers themselves – the authors of this book.

Many, many people go through life dreaming of having something published, of making a statement or telling a tale. For most, it remains no more than a dream, an unfulfilled ambition. But for the authors in this volume that dream is now a reality, proving that they're the best – they're not just the bee's knees, they're also the cat's pyjamas!

Dr Pat Donlon,
Chairperson, Jury

Contents

ABC, Vicky Dillon 9
The Hungry Vacuum Cleaner, Niamh ní Ghallchóir 10
The Spider, Deirdre ní Mhuirthile 15
Milltowncross, Stephen Bennett 16
War, Michael Ross 22
An Taibhse, Tomás Ó Spealláin 24
M.E. and Me, Kathy Clifford 25
Eating an Apple, Graham Mullane 31
An Páistín, Séamus de Nais 32
The Robber, Suzanne Rath 33
Rary, Doireann ní Ghríofa 37
When I Grow Up, Sarah Aherne 39
Mo Pheann Draíochta, Séamus de Nais 40
The Ballad of Mary Whyte, Eimear Lynch 42
An Taibhse, Dylan Ó Searcaí 44
Dew in a Cobweb, Daire Mac Raois 46
Snow, Daire Mac Raois 47
The Lonely Fox, Emily Egan 48
An Guthán, Bríd de Faoite 51
Beidh Mé Ann, Hilda Flynn 52
The Exodus from Ireland, Michael O'Sullivan 55
The Day the Dust Blew In, Layla O'Mara 56
Oil, Saba Rahmani 63

Last Christmas, Sarah Ryan 65
My Doggie, Emma Long 68
My Home, Cliodhna Martin 68
James's Quest, Seamus O'Brien 69
Life on a Farm, Anna-Marie Higgins 78
A Shark Called Bugsy Brown, Alison McClelland 81
Trees in Winter, Rahmona Henry 82
Trees, Miriam Sweeney 83
The Quest of the Sarakai, Mark Fottrell 84
An Tuaisceart, Niall mac Innéirí 92
Don't Worry, Be Yourself, Ruth Finneran 93
The Friendly Giant, Emer Delaney 99
Avenging the Grape, Geraldine Hayes 101
Am Taistil, Dara de Búrca 108
The Crab, Gillian McCusker 111
The Duck, Gillian McCusker 112
The Snail, Isobel Abbott 113
Saol Mogwa, Miriam nic Artúir 114
Rain, Peter Killian 116
The Tale of a Goblin, Ruth Mac Namara 117
Oceania, Flower of the Deep, Una Harnett 118
Peig Sayers, Kathleen Treacy 123
My Brother and The Ship, Alice Hamilton 125
A Gruesome Discovery, Peter Durkan 126
An Cúl, Aoife ní Ghliasáin 129
I Believe, Neal Brophy 130
An Dara Seans, Aoife ní Ghliasáin 131
The Pink Mini and Ruler, Bernard Kealy 137
A First Job, Martin Hehir 138

List of Contributors 150

ABC

VICKY DILLON

Michael learned his ABC
But he learned it just as far as E.
So G H I J and K would have to wait
another day.
They might have to wait another
month or so.
Perhaps a year, I don't know.

In fact I think
In fact I know
He still has not got to O.

The Hungry Vacuum Cleaner

NIAMH NÍ GHALLCHÓIR

We suspected nothing until the morning the cat was gone. We had just got a new security system fitted. All the windows were blocked, all the doors were locked, there was no way in, there was no way out, there was no cat. We searched, we searched, and kept on searching. Up the chimney, in the washing machine, under the sink, behind the wardrobe and finally we looked in the cupboard under the stairs. But alas, all that was there was our new bright red hoover that had arrived in a big box three weeks earlier labelled 'HANDLE WITH CARE'. When we opened the box we saw a bright red shiny hoover with silver trimming and a silver snout that twisted and turned like a snake.

On Tuesday Mum decided to try the hoover. It worked, but when she went to turn it off she stepped on the flex and suddenly it coiled up around her leg. She screamed and my older brother ran in to help her. He was astonished to see what had happened and quick as lightning he uncoiled the flex.

That was two weeks after the cat disappeared and everyone had forgotten about it except me. I had come to the conclusion that the cat had escaped out a window before we locked up. But I still was a tiny bit suspicious.

The next day I became even more suspicious than ever because three more things had disappeared, the kettle, my violin bow, and the portrait of my great grandfather that had been hanging on the sittingroom wall.

On his way to work my father reported the mysterious happenings and the police too were bewildered. The next day nothing strange happened, nor the next day, nor any day of the following week. But on Thursday morning when we got up the new television was gone. Now this was too much. We decided that each night someone would keep watch. First it was Dad, then me, then my older brother, and last my Mum.

I couldn't wait. I hoped I would catch the thief. If I did I might be famous. I might even be on the news, or better still, in the headlines. I can just imagine it: 'Pamela Walsh catches world's greatest thief, Burglar Bill!' Well, I had to wait a whole night and what if Dad caught him first?

Next morning I woke up at six o'clock and went downstairs to see had Dad caught the thief. But when I got down, what a sight met my eyes! Dad was fast asleep on the stairs. I shook him and he woke with a start.

'Did you catch the thief?' I asked him.

'Thief, what thief?' he answered sleepily.

'The thief you stayed up to catch,' I said.

'Oh, that thief, no, no I didn't. I fell asleep, but do you know, I had the most wonderful dream. I dreamt that I …'

'Be quiet. You won't be getting this job again. Tonight I'm going to catch that thief if it's the last thing I do,' I said.

'Well, I'm going to bed, are you?' he asked.

'No, I'm going to see if anything has disappeared.'

I looked in the diningroom. The Lego was gone. Oh no! My brothers would be disappointed. But that would be the last thing that would disappear if I had anything to do with it.

The next night 11 o'clock came and Mum and Dad went to bed. I was the only one awake. I was going to catch that thief. I sat at the bottom of the stairs with my torch. I decided not to turn on my torch until I heard something. I had had a sleep during the day so I wasn't tired.

I waited and waited and I nearly gave up hope, until finally at a quarter to four I heard a kind of snort. I immediately flicked on my torch. I shone it where I had heard the snort. I nearly fainted. There right in front of me was the new *vacuum cleaner* eating a lampshade. The top of its snout turned into an evil eye and stared at me. Then it started to snarl. It moved closer to me. I dodged and stood on the end of the snout! The hoover made a choking sound and then the snout dropped. There was silence.

I ran upstairs and woke Mum and Dad. At first they didn't believe me, but when they saw the half-eaten lampshade they were very surprised.

'Well, I'm ringing the guards to tell them the case is solved,' said Dad. 'And we had better get rid of that hoover. It hasn't brought anything but trouble.'

So the next day when we all woke up, we put the hoover back in its box and drove it straight to the dog pound.

We knew it was dead. But we couldn't be too sure.

The Spider

DEIRDRE NÍ MHUIRTHILE

Silver threads among the gold,
a solitary chain,
a little silent spider climbs
and dives down again.
The gold stalks sway,
the spider plummets
earthwards; she drops her stitch of silver.

A time passes, then
once again she tries;
perseverance her best quality.
With skill and grace,
she weaves an intricate chain,
unnoticed and unrewarded.

But she is satisfied;
proud of her skilful art,
she noiselessly descends and crawls away.

The next morning a beautiful necklace
of dewdrops in the field
was looked upon by a critic.
'A simple spider made that,' said he,
'and no wonder – some stitches are out of place.'

Milltowncross

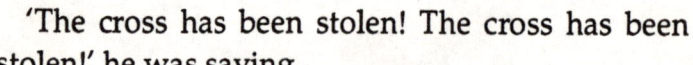
STEPHEN BENNETT

Everything was buzzing in Milltowncross. Nothing unusual was happening, just everybody going about their daily business. Then old Johnny the carpenter saw a figure running down the hill towards the town. He was stumbling and falling and yelling something at the top of his voice, which nobody could hear. Johnny recognised him as Mick the shepherd, who was usually up on the hill minding sheep.

When he got to the town a crowd gathered around him.

'The cross has been stolen! The cross has been stolen!' he was saying.

A gasp went around the crowd. Somebody went and got the mayor. When he heard, he nearly fainted. A long time passed before everybody was calm.

Mick told his story of how he found out about the cross. He had gone up on the hill to count the sheep when he noticed that the cross was gone.

The mayor decided to have a search. Everybody in the town looked in every nook and cranny in the whole place. Strong man Big Jimmy even pulled up all the grass and looked under it. But the search came to no result and they all went home sad.

The next day everybody went about their business miserably. The mayor had called in Inspector Sidbottom, but he was no use in raising anybody's hopes since the only case he had ever

solved was the case of the missing penny chewing gum.

Then the town dunce rushed out on the street with a cross in his hand. But when people found out that this cross came from the church, they gave him a thump and he went home to his mother, crying.

Then the mayor decided to Tippex out any sign of the cross in the whole town. Everybody was given a bottle of Tippex and soon there was no sign of a cross anywhere.

As time went by people began to like the name Milltown and when the mayor saw this he decided to hold a party and a play to celebrate the town's new name. Preparations began. The mayor went around and told people the wrong things to do and just generally got in the way. When finally everything was ready they sent out invitations to all the neighbouring towns. It was to be a fancy dress so everybody was busy ordering their costumes from the local costume shop. (They were lucky because there just happened to be a costume shop opened in the town by one of the committee.)

The night of the party arrived and people came in every costume, from Alfred Hitchcock to Queen Elizabeth the Second. The party began and just when the play was going well, out on the stage

jumped Fred Maguo, yelling something which nobody could hear because his head was in a horse's costume.

The mayor and a few other people went up on the stage to find out what was going on. They tried to get the horse's head off but the zip got stuck and it was several minutes before they managed it. When they did, Fred started yelling: 'The mill has been stolen! The mill has been stolen!' A gasp went around the hall and a lot of young girls with weak nerves fainted.

Inspector Sidbottom arrived on the stage but when somebody saw him they threw him off. After a while calm was restored and everybody asked Fred what had happened. Seemingly he had got too hot in the hall and had gone out for some fresh air. Then he saw that the mill was gone. The people of the town and the visitors went out and searched, but found nothing.

Again everybody was given a bottle of Tippex and they went around and Tippexed out any sign of the mill. The next day they all went around humiliated at the name of the town, but in years to come there were benefits from it. They got a prize for the silliest name for a town and they got one for the weirdest sign, which was 'WELCOME TO TOWN'.

War

MICHAEL ROSS

Old war,
Horses neighing
Swords humming
Death screams
Sunlight glinting
On blades
1700's war
Musket shots
Smoke.

More death screams
Again swords
New war
Nuclear bombs
Machine gun chatter
Flashing bayonets
ICBMs
Countries spend billions.
War
Women weeping
Children crying
For husbands and fathers, asking
Why?

An Taibhse

TOMÁS Ó SPEALLÁIN

Oíche amháin
is mise i mo shuí,
chuala mé torann –
ó mo chroí!

Anuas an simléir
a tháinig sé
starrfhiacail is fuil –
bhí mo chroí i mo bhéal.

Bhéic mé is scréach mé
do mo shaol!
ach ansin go tobann,
dhúisigh mé.

M.E. and Me

KATHY CLIFFORD

My name is Kathy Clifford. I'm twelve years old. I have blue eyes and dark brown hair. I have M.E. and I'm not at school at the moment. I haven't really been at school since the middle of February 1991 and it is now September 7th 1991. I miss school a lot.

I can't go to school because I can't walk. I can't walk because my legs are too sore to stand on and I get tired very easily. The glands in my arms and neck are very sore at the moment too, so is my throat, and I have a headache and I am very tired today. All these things are part of having M.E. You get good days and bad. Today is a bad day for me because I'm so tired.

I've been to a lot of doctors and healers. Not many doctors believe in M.E. because it does not show up in blood tests. I was lucky to have a doctor who did believe in it. Rest is the only thing that helps. I've also been to bio-energy. They were very nice and they said that they would try to make me better. I have been there four times now and I don't feel any better.

I'm going to a man who teaches people Christian meditation. I have to do it three times a day, which is a bit of a drag because I don't always feel like doing it.

I'm going to a specialist doctor too. He mostly works with people who have M.E. He is giving me injections. He has also put me on a lot of vitamins. I have to take thirteen every day.

10.9.1991

It's Tuesday the 10th of September. I am sitting in my mum's bed now. It's 10.30 a.m. and I've just finished doing my Irish. I'm going to listen to the radio and draw for a while. Bríd, who comes to teach me, comes at four. She's only supposed to stay for an hour but she usually stays until 5.30. I know she's being nice but I don't always think it's so nice. I'm in my mum's bed because I didn't feel like getting up and there's a phone beside her bed. My aunt and Granny ring me every day.

11.9.1991

I was at the doctor today. I got another injection. Afterwards my mum had to go to the bank. I waited at the top of the stairs. There was a lady sitting on a bench. She smiled over at me all the time. I'm very conscious of people looking at me even though most of the time they are not.

12.9.1991

It's 2 o'clock now. I've been going around in circles with a pen in my mouth and listening to the radio and singing along with the songs I know and thinking about what to write. I'm very tired today. I didn't get to sleep last night until 2 o'clock and I woke up four times.

14.9.1991

When I was in the video shop today, two little boys came up to my mum and said, 'What happened to your little girl?' My mum said, 'Ask her', and then I said, 'I fell' and they went away. I wish people would ignore the fact that I'm in a wheelchair, but that would probably hurt more. Sometimes I wish I had my legs wrapped up in very noticeable fat bandages so people wouldn't automatically think I was handicapped.

15.9.1991

Today's Sunday. I haven't done anything or been anywhere yet. I tried to stand up today. I'm still not able. It's half-two now. I'm looking out our patio door. I have been for the last thirty minutes. The wind is making ripples in the grass and the leaves on our little red tree in the corner of the garden are beating up and down like birds' wings. Every few minutes the light on the garden changes as the clouds pass across in front of the sun. The wind seems to have stopped now and everything is silent except the sound of me rocking backwards and forwards in my wheelchair.

The wind is blowing again. I don't like silence. It gives me too much time to think. A little while ago a cat came in to the garden. I don't like that cat because he jumped in through our open kitchen on Friday night and when I came in I got an awful shock. Anyway I kept banging on the patio door until he went to my neighbour's garden. There was a man I didn't know standing in their garden. I think he thought I was banging at him. Then I closed the curtains and went over the other side and peeped out. He was gone.

17.9.1991

Today is Tuesday. I feel awful today. I'm very tired and very sore. My neck, throat, head, arms and all down my legs are very sore. I have a cold too, and all the stuff from my nose is trickling slowly down my throat. It stings like mad.

19.9.1991

It's Thursday. I don't feel like doing anything now. Bríd gave me a book I could read if I got bored. I was just looking at it. It's called *An Bheanbh Bhig* and it's a very very long version of 'The Three Little Pigs'. It's in Irish. I read five chapters of it during the summer. It's a very boring book. It has two hundred pages and no pictures and the print is very small.

27.9.1991

Today is Friday. It is 1.15 p.m. There are a lot of birds singing. My next-door neighbours must be cleaning their chimney or something. They're making a lot of noise. I can hear them walking around upstairs in their house. When I had a cough after Christmas 1990 they said I used to wake them up at night. I can hear a lot of noises in my house too. Not big noises, just little creaking sounds. My mum says they are settling noises. It sounds like somebody tiptoeing around. I used to think there might be burglars in my house. It's scary sometimes to think I can't run away. I couldn't get out of my house myself because the steps are too big to get my wheelchair down. Unless I crawled down and then pulled my wheelchair down after me, but my wheelchair is very heavy. A few weeks ago I was listening to the radio. They were talking about poltergeists. It means there are spirits going around your house, but they don't do you any harm.

28.9.1991

Today is Saturday.

Not many shops have lifts. I think every shop with an upstairs should have a lift or some way for people in wheelchairs to see what is upstairs. They have just as much right to be there as everybody else. Before I couldn't walk I didn't think or care very much about people in wheelchairs. I just looked away quickly and ignored them. I know this sounds mean but I couldn't help it. I did it automatically, which is no excuse. When I started to use my wheelchair I didn't want to go out. A lot of people did the same thing I did, they looked and then they looked away very quickly. Some people stared and some people acted normally. I felt angry at the people who looked away or stared. A lot of people think because your legs don't work neither does your brain. That was always what I thought, but it's not true. I think my attitude to people in wheelchairs has changed, and to handicapped people.

30.9.1991

Today is Monday.

It is 2 o'clock. It's a very dreamy kind of day. I miss school a lot. I can't wait to be back. I only have to get two more injections. Not everybody who gets the injections gets better. Four out of five people get cured. I hope I'm one of them.

Eating an Apple

GRAHAM MULLANE

*My apple looks like a
cricket ball.
It feels cold and sticky.
It smells like grass in the summer.
It sounds like crunching a tayto and it
tastes very sweet.
When I swallow it my mouth
feels cold.*

An Páistín

SÉAMUS DE NAIS

Tá páistín againn sa bhaile.
Eilís is ainm di.
Bíonn sí ag súgradh, is ag spraoi,
istigh agus amuigh.

Níl ach dhá bhliain aici,
ach is cladhaire í gach lá.
Cuireann sí gach rud i bhfolach,
ach fós bíonn sí lán de ghrá.

I rith na hoíche dorcha,
dúisíonn sí sinn go léir,
le béicíl agus caoineadh,
mar go bhfeiceann sí rud sa spéir!

Caitheann sí éadaí galánta,
ón siopa atá againn,
agus uaireanta canann sí mar Kylie,
ach i ndáiríre níl a guth binn!

Sin í mo dheirfiúr Eilís.
Lán de spraoi is lán de ghrá,
is breá linn go bhfuil sí sa teach againn,
san oíche is sa lá!

The Robber

S U Z A N N E   R A T H

Once upon a time there lived an old woman. She lived in a forest far away from any village, town or city. She loved animals and birds and they loved her. Every day they came to her for food. She lived on water, nuts and eggs. Her hens laid beautiful eggs. The squirrel supplied her with nuts from his store and she got the water from a well nearby. She had the most beautiful garden you have ever seen even if it was made with wild flowers. Her house was nearly hidden by evergreen trees.

One day she put on her hat and set off to the squirrel's tree to get some nuts. But bad news was waiting for her. The squirrel had not got any nuts left.

'You took the last lot last week,' he explained. 'I am very sorry but our spring crop of nuts is not ripe yet and will not be until February.'

'This is indeed bad news, Mr Squirrel,' said the old woman. 'I will have to go and find food because my hens are not laying and I cannot live on water for a month.' So she set off.

She walked for forty-seven miles until she reached the nearest village. She knocked on a door. A woman opened it. When she heard what the old woman wanted she replied, 'I have no food to give you but take this crystal ball. Everything you ask for, it will give you.'

The old woman went home happy. She left the crystal ball on the table while she went to get water. But when she came back it was gone.

'Oh dear,' she sighed, 'I will have to go and see that woman again.'

So once again she had a drink of water and she set off. When the woman heard what had happened to her crystal ball she was very sad. She thought for a minute, then she said, 'You must have a robber, but I know how you can catch him. Come inside and I will tell you.'

So the old woman went inside with her and sat down.

'First of all,' said the woman, 'as you have had your crystal ball stolen I will give you this tablecloth. Whenever you say, "tablecloth, tablecloth make me some food", the tablecloth will at once obey you and it will supply you with the most delicious food for as long as you like. And now,' she added, 'now I will tell you how to catch the robber. The robber will want to steal that tablecloth that I have just given you. So I know how to catch him. I have got some string and honey. I will give it to you because you will need it. Tonight you must leave your kitchen window open. You must dip this string into the honey. Then you must wind the string round the kitchen window that you left open. When the robber gets caught in the sticky string, the police will come and catch him.'

The old woman went home and did as she was told. That night the robber was caught and the old woman lived happily ever after.

Rary

DOIREANN NÍ GHRÍOFA

Lá amháin, bhí Niamh ag siúl sa choill, nuair a chuala sí torann. Ó áit éigin taobh thiar de sceach a bhí sé ag teacht. Shiúil sí anonn go dtí an sceach agus d'fhéach sí taobh thiar di. Bhí ubh an-mhór ann. Bhí scoilt mhór san ubh. Ní raibh aon éan sa timpeall agus gheobhadh an t-éinín istigh san ubh bás mura dtabharfadh sí léi é.

Choimeád sí é in aice leis an tine. Faoi dheireadh tháinig an t-éan amach as an ubh, agus bhí sé an-mhór! Nuair a bhí sé dhá lá d'aois, bhí sé chomh mór le cathaoir. Nuair a bhí an t-éan dhá sheachtain d'aois, ní raibh Niamh in ann an t-éan a choinneáil ina rún níos mó.

Fuair a Mamaí amach faoi, nuair a chonaic sí Niamh ag rith timpeall an chlóis, i ndiaidh éin a bhí beagnach chomh mór léi féin. Nuair a tháinig Daidí Niamh abhaile dúirt Mamaí leis é.

Bhí an-suim ag Daidí Niamh san éan. Fuair sé amach an t-ainm a bhí air ó dhuine de na cairde a bhí aige. Seo an t-ainm a bhí air: Arbicouscarblabhasium.

Ach cheap Niamh go raibh an t-ainm sin ró-fhada, agus rinne sí suas ainm eile dó, 'Rary', mar go raibh sé an-'*rare*'.

Bhí eagla ar mháthair Niamh roimh an éan agus bhí plean aici chun é a mharú. Lá amháin, nuair a bhí Niamh ar scoil chuir a Mam glaoch fóin ar chara léi (ní raibh a fhios ag Mam go raibh an Rary in ann caint!).

Tháinig an cara, agus bhí 'DUMP TRUCK' mór aige. Thóg sé an t-éan go dtí an dump ansin. An nóiméad a bhí an cara chun an Rary a chaitheamh isteach sa tip, thosaigh an Rary ag canadh: 'It's a Long Way to Tip-a-Rary!'

Baineadh geit mhór as an tiománaí agus stop sé de bheith ag tiomáint an DUMP TRUCK ar feadh soicind. Ag an soicind sin rith Niamh isteach, agus thóg sí an Rary. Rith sí abhaile chomh tapaidh is ab fhéidir léi. Bhí a cairde ag fanacht léi. D'inis sí dóibh céard a tharla don Rary. An lá ina dhiaidh sin, rinne siad go léir teach beag don Rary agus cloisim go bhfuil sé fós ina chónaí ann!

When I Grow Up

SARAH AHERNE

Growing up. Growing up is when your face gets bigger, your hair gets longer and you grow taller. When you grow up you leave your parents and have your own house.

When I grow up I want to be a vet. What a vet does is that he or she helps animals that are sick and dying. I love all animals, even dangerous animals. I have a special love for horses but it's not good for me because I've got asthma – it's really the hay that's not good for me.

I want to have a small house because only I'll be living in it. I am not going to get married and have kids because I wouldn't have time to be with them.

I am thinking of going to boarding-school. I have to finish national school first. In secondary school I hope to get good marks in my Inter Cert and my Leaving Cert.

I have a long way to go yet. I am only nine years old but I hope to have a good career and will always try to help animals.

Mo Pheann Draíochta

SÉAMUS DE NAIS

Fuair mé peann ó mo Mham inné
mar bhronntanas do mo breithlá
bhí sé dearg is glas, glan is glé,
agus líon mo shúile le grá.

Chuir mé isteach i mo mhála é,
ionas go mbeadh sé slán
is nuair a chuaigh mé ar scoil
bhí mo pheann draíochta bán!

Thóg mé amach go sciobtha é,
is d'fhéach mé air faoi dhó
cheap mé gur chuala mé ag caint é,
ag rá, 'hippity hoppity ho'!

Chaith mé suas san aer é,
is nuair a tháinig sé anuas
léim sé ar mo ghualainn,
is chuir sé cogar i mo chluas.

*'Beidh mé mar chara duitse,
cabhróidh mé leat go deo
beimid iontach le chéile,
fad a bheidh an bheirt againn beo!'*

*Is ansin a mhothaigh mé rud éigin —
léim mé suas de phreab
mo Mham a bhí os mo chomhair amach
ina suí ar mo chathaoir gan cead!*

*Ghlaoigh mé ar mo pheann draíochta,
chun seasamh ar an bhfód!
ach ní raibh sa seomra ach beirt againn,
is bhí mise ag brionglóid!*

The Ballad of Mary Whyte

EIMEAR LYNCH

There was a girl called Mary Whyte,
Who wouldn't learn to read and write.
The teachers in schools everywhere
Gave up on her in deep despair.
Mary simply would not learn.
She was the cause of much concern.
'You have to learn to read,' they said,
But Mary simply shook her head.
'You are not right. There is no need
For me to learn to write and read,'
She proclaimed with great conviction.
But this, of course, was only fiction.

*One day she went out for a stroll,
But didn't see a great big hole.
The hole was deep and dark and scary,
But escaped the eyes of foolish Mary.
There was a sign that clearly showed
'BEWARE OF BIG HOLE IN THE ROAD'.
But the notice Mary didn't heed,
Because she hadn't learned to read.
Down she fell with a noisy shriek,
And wasn't rescued for a week.*

*In hospital, with her head in plaster,
'What happened to you?' her friends all asked her.
'I fell down a big, dark hole,' she said,
'I wish I'd learned to read instead!'*

*That's the sad tale of Mary Whyte.
(Make sure that YOU can read and write!)*

An Taibhse

DYLAN Ó SEARCAÍ

An bhliain seo caite, Mí Iúil, chuaigh mé go Coláiste Gaeilge i gCo. na Gaillimhe. Coláiste Lurgan an t-ainm a bhí ar an gColáiste. Bhí céilí ar siúl oíche amháin. Thosaigh sé ag a hocht a chlog. Bhí sé go hiontach. Ach ní raibh sé go hiontach nuair a bhí mé ag dul abhaile. Bhí sé an-dorcha.

Bhí mé ag fanacht le mo sheanathair agus mo sheanmháthair i gcarbhán. Bhí an carbhán suite in áit álainn, thíos ar an gcladach. Bhí bóithrín fada ag dul ón gColáiste go dtí an cladach. Ar an taobh chlé, leath slí síos, tá reilig mhór. Téann cosán síos ó bharr na reilige. Bhí timpeall fiche coca féir tirim sa reilig.

Nuair a bhí mé ag geata na reilige thosaigh coca féir ag siúl. De phreab na súl tháinig neart i mo chosa. Rith mé ar nós na gaoithe go dtí an carbhán. Ní raibh anáil fágtha agam. Níor thit mé i mo chodladh go gceann cúpla uair leis an ngeit a bain sé asam.

Lá arna mhárach bhí mo sheanmháthair ag insint an scéil don bhean a bhí ina cónaí ag barr bhóithrín na reilige. Thosaigh sí ag gáire. 'M'fhear céile a bhí ann,' a deir sise. 'Bhí sé ag siúl le píce lán d'fhéar tirim thar a cheann. Ní raibh ach a chosa le feiceáil agus bhí sé cosúil le coca féir. Sin an taibhse a chonaic do gharmhac.'

Dew in a Cobweb

DAIRE MAC RAOIS

In the fields grass
sparkles
and sweet pollen fills
the air, and
in a thorn bush
like a diamond
is the spider's
lair.

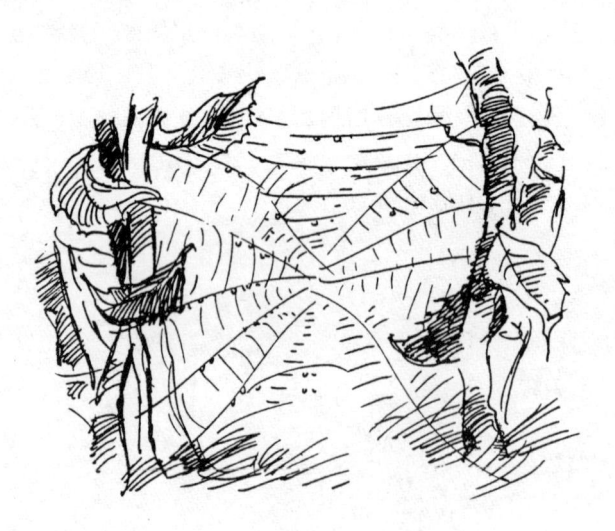

Snow

DAIRE MAC RAOIS

A big cloud looms over
the sky
an invisible pin bursts
the cloud
and small white
parachutes
float to the ground.

The Lonely Fox

EMILY EGAN

It was a warm night. Vixen peeped from behind the bunch of dead nettles in front of her den. The coast was clear. Earlier she had decided to hunt in the farm over the hill. She usually hunted in her own wood so this would be a change. It was a year since her mate had been shot in that farm. Yet she remembered it so clearly. The shot and then the yelp of pain from the dying animal. She would never forget that moment, never.

Suddenly the pangs of hunger shook Vixen into reality. She started to trot cautiously out of the woods. She looked back over her shoulder and saw the woods shimmering silver in the moonlight. A rabbit scurried in among the trees as the fox approached. She then trotted on over the hill and halted at the large bush, remembering the past. The memory seemed to give her courage. Lifting her tail she fearlessly made her way into that very farmyard itself. Just then a chicken wandered past and in the flicker of an eyelid she sprang. All the lights flashed on and the alarm went off. Vixen found herself exposed in the middle of a large farmyard. She frantically scanned the scene for some cover. Just as she decided to retreat to the bush she had just passed, the farmyard door burst open and a large scowling man ran out carrying a shotgun.

The man took aim and fired. A deafening sound filled the night air as the pellets whizzed menacingly towards the terrified vixen. With heart pounding she made a desperate lunge towards the bush.

For one brief happy moment Vixen thought she was safe, but just as she reached the bush a burning pain shot up her hind leg. The pain was so agonising she could hardly breathe. Her beautiful fur was clogged and matted by the pumping blood. Vixen knew she would never see her home in the wood again. She also knew the dogs would soon come to tear her apart. A silent sob swelled up in her throat as she looked up at the clear starry sky. She could hear the dogs yelping excitedly as the farmer fumbled with the bolt on the farm door. Sadly she thought of how her mate must have gone through the same thing just a year before.

The barking of the dogs grew louder. The terrified vixen cried silently. She had lost so much blood that she was feeling weak. Then to her amazement the pain suddenly seemed to leave her wounded leg. The light around her started to fade. In the distance a bright light appeared. It grew and grew until it blazed in splendour and in the very centre stood her mate.

He beckoned to her to follow him. A peaceful feeling washed over her whole body as she rose. Everything else was gone as she followed her mate into the light of the second life.

An Guthán

BRÍD DE FAOITE

Tá gléas againn sa teach,
Is ba mhaith le mo mháthair é a dhó,
Bíonn gach éinne á úsáid,
San oíche is sa ló.

Is dócha gur buntáiste é
Ar shlí amháin nó dhó nó trí!
Is féidir liom a bheith ag caint,
Le m'aintín i mBá Bheanntraí.

Is gléas teagmhála é,
A úsáideadh blianta ó shin,
San am sin b'áis an-mhór
É a bheith agat i do thig.

Is é an gléas dá bhfuilim ag tagairt,
Dár ndóigh an rógaire guthán,
Agus is amhlaidh go bhfuil sé san am seo
Chomh coitianta le harán bán.

Beidh Mé Ann

HILDA FLYNN

Bhris ar an bhfoighne agam. Anois nó riamh, a dúirt mé liom féin. Isteach liom sa seomra agus phioc mé suas an teileafón. Dhiailigh mé an uimhir go tapaidh agus d'fhan mé go dtí gur phioc duine suas an teileafón ar an taobh eile. Tar éis cúpla soicind, bhí mé ag caint leis. Cheap mé go raibh nóta brónach ina ghuth ach níor bhac mé leis mar bhí mé ar buile.

'Cén fáth nár chuir tú fios orm, a Dherry? Dúirt tú leathuair tar éis a naoi. Tá sé cúig chun a haon déag anois.'

'Tá an-bhrón orm ach tá rud uafásach tar éis tarlú. Tá mo mháthair marbh.'

'Cad a tharla?'

'Buaileadh tinn í, go gearr i ndiaidh di an dinnéar a ithe. Tháinig an dochtúir agus dúirt sé go mbeadh sí ceart go leor tar éis codladh mhaith. Ach fuair sí bás tamaillín roimh a deich a chlog. Ó, a Dhia! Cad a dhéanfaidh mé?' a dúirt sé agus é ag caoineadh.

Is beag nár thosaigh mé féin ag caoineadh freisin. Bhí mé tar éis a bheith ag tabhairt amach dó agus bhí a mháthair marbh. Ba bhreá liom dá slogfadh an talamh mé. Bhí a fhios ag a mhuintir le trí mhí anuas go raibh galar croí ar Bhean Uí Chonaill. Ach tháinig an bás aniar aduaidh orthu ar fad anois.

'Ó, Dherry! Tá brón orm. Ní raibh a fhios agam. An bhfuil aon rud gur féidir liom a dhéanamh duit?'

'Ná bí buartha fúmsa. Níl aon rud uaim ach tamall gearr le bheith i m'aonar.'

'Tuigim. Cathain a bheidh an tsochraid?'

'Nílim cinnte. Ach tráthnóna amárach, b'fhéidir.'

'Ceart go leor. Feicfidh mé thú amárach.'

'Ceart go leor. Slán.'

'Slán.'

Chuaigh mé go dtí mo sheomra ach níor chodail mé go sámh. Bhí mé ag smaoineamh ar Dherry agus ar a mhuintir chroíbhriste.

An mhaidin dar gcionn chuaigh mé go dtí teach Dherry. Ní raibh sé ann, agus ní raibh a fhios ag a athair cá raibh sé. Ach bhí a fhios agamsa. Ag an áit chéanna a théann sé nuair a bhíonn aon rud cearr leis. Sea gan dabht, bhí sé ann. Ag barr na páirce móire, taobh thiar dá theach. Shuigh mé síos in aice leis. D'fhéadfadh duine an baile iomlán a fheiceáil ón áit seo.

'Bhí a fhios agat cá raibh mé,' a dúirt sé.

'Is ansin a bhíonn tú i gcónaí nuair nach mbíonn tú ag féachaint ar an teilifís.'

Thug mé faoi deara nach raibh sé an-bhrónach ar fad. Cinnte, ní raibh sé in ardghiúmar ach oiread. Ach bhí a fhios agam nach raibh ann ach cur i gcéill.

I nduibheagán a chroí, bhí sé uaigneach. Ba é buachaill bán a Mham é.

'Tá áthas orm gur tháinig tú inniu. Go raibh maith agat,' a dúirt sé.

'Ní fhéadfainn tú a fhágaint i d'aonar ag falróid timpeall na háite.'

Thiontaigh sé chugam agus leathgháire faiteach ar a bhéal.

'Go raibh maith agat arís.'

> *D'aithníomar uaigneas a chéile*
> *Is d'éisteamar le chéile*
> *Le cogarnaíl na gcrann.*
> *D'ólamar an bháisteach*
> *agus thuigeamar a chéile*
> *Is d'aithníomar an tuiscint.*

The Exodus from Ireland

MICHAEL O'SULLIVAN

And a wave broke on the shore,
and the woman looked west.
She knew she would see them no more,
for they had gone with the rest.
The breaking of the waves,
the howling of the wind,
the screeching of the gulls as they soared by
  the caves,
and with a sigh she turned to go,
'Slán,' she said, 'Slán go deo.'

The Day the Dust Blew In

LAYLA O'MARA

'As birds were born to fly, people were born to be free'
Unknown

San Antonio
17 April 1898

In some ways it all seems such a long time ago and at others the scars seem all too fresh. But deep down there has always been a dark cloud hanging over my past. It was and always will be a stab through my heart, but I need to uncover and plough through my dark past. I was young then and life was carefree. I didn't know life was ever different. This diary is to try to clear my own mind and anyone else's who cares to read it.

Atar, Africa
23 May 1879

The sun had just risen in the hot summer sky. It was early and Mamma, Baba and Ndeoma were still fast asleep. I lay looking out of the open door, the antelope skin blowing in the breeze. The low row of lemon grass wavering to and fro, its sweet smell wafting about the room. But then on the horizon I noticed a cloud of dust advancing.

'Baba,' I called, 'look, look.'

Baba rose from his bed still half in a dream world where nothing went wrong. We stood in a group huddled around the doorway. All eyes were set on the ever closer dust.

What, Baba, what is it? I wanted to ask, but Baba looked so old as his wise brow wrinkled with worry.

'Ndekpo, Ndeoma, hide *now*!' he snapped.

'Why, Baba?' I had to ask.

'Don't ask questions, just do it!' His voice trembled.

Through the open door I saw that the mysterious dust had closed in on us. The dust was men brandishing sharp and hard stones and sticks set alight. The evil flames snapped and crackled. I lay there in a daze. What was happening?

The smell of smoke closing my lungs shook me from my dazed state. Everywhere – all around the huts that had been our home, our shelter – was engulfed with flames. The furniture carefully made by Baba, the woven clothes and mats of Mamma's and the palm-tree roofs all blazed and burned before my eyes. Then Mamma's screams filled the air, my ears and head. As I write this I can still hear her shouting out in desperation. A man stood over her, beating her mercilessly. Mamma struggled, lashed out, but the heavy club kept hitting over and over again. Suddenly her piercing screams died away. It has taken me until now to accept this, but poor dear Mamma was brutally and blood-thirstily murdered.

End of June

We were at sea floating over a mass of unknown blue, to an unknown destination among unknown people. Crated like cattle, treated like dogs and spoken to like beasts, I truly believed I had been sent to hell for my wrong-doings.

For weeks I slept and barely ate in a confined space with hardly any room to move or breathe. Many died from lack of air. For weeks on end I saw people all around, children and adults, fade away. Like flies, people died. Each day piles of bodies were thrown out to sea, their graves amongst the seaweed and fish. I am sure if a carefree person were to set foot upon that deadly ship their life would be heavily burdened, and no happiness could remove it.

At times I nearly gave up this world, but what was the point? I was already in hell, wasn't I? Alas, Baba saw that the boat wasn't hell, but a brutal injustice. He silently died.

So now, Ndeoma and I were left alone without a Mamma or Baba. Both were murdered. Just a few weeks before, life was simple and now? Now we were stuck in a harsh, unfair world.

July

Ndeoma lay beside me stone cold. As I took her hand I felt as though a chunk of me had been torn away. Now Ndeoma too had died because of a terrible crime. The daily collection of the dead bodies began. I clung on to Ndeoma as if she was a part of me. I didn't want her to leave. This must be a dream, a horrible nightmare – but no, and now I was left all alone.

End of July

'Come on, 'ere's a fine boy. Look at those arms, a born worker. Open yer mouth, nigger, come on.'

A rough, unshaven white man yanked my mouth open and showed the sea of white people my 'strong fine clampers'.

'This boy, I happen to know, is a smart one. He'll work in the house if ye train him. Who'll give me a starting price?'

'One dollar, sir.'

'Come on, any higher?'

'One dollar fifty.'

'Two, two over 'ere.'

'Three, sir.'

'Three dollars fifty.'

'Four fifty.'

'Come on, now.'

five dollars.'

'Any advance on five? No, no, yes.'

'Five dollars fifty.'

'Going once, twice, three times – *gone!*'

A hammer slammed down loud and hard. I was sold.

August

For mile upon mile we marched chained together under the hot sun. My master beat us till the ground turned reddish pink.

After about a week of travelling we arrived at a large house surrounded by an even bigger farm. But that obviously was not for us slaves. Shacks, dark and smoky, were my living quarters for four long years.

'Crack!' A whip lashed around my ears.

'Get a move on,' Montgomery roared.

'I can't, Master.'

'Can't? Course ya can.'

'No, Mas'.'

'Right, Nigger.' Mas' threw his whip at me. 'You whip 'em.'

WHAT – HIT MY OWN PEOPLE?

'Hard,' Mas' roared.

After about a week I learnt the tricks of the trade. Firstly you cracked the whip in the air, bringing it down near the victim's back, but before reaching it you jerked the whip back. The victim then shouted out in pain, pretending to be hurt though they really hadn't been touched. Mas' never found out our tricks, thank God.

Many, many incidents stand out in my mind, all similar to those of any other black person, but there is one so awful and unfair that I have to write it down on paper. I think it shows perfectly the violent cruelty we were subjected to.

Mas' Montgomery wasn't one to see anyone resting or any time being wasted. The cotton season (August) was hard and long, and Mas' was harsh. Women with little babies had to work regardless. All the babies were left in a big trough for the day. On one such day all of us were working hard. The air felt humid and sticky and on the skyline black clouds were coming in fast. Soon they were in on top of us. The rain pelted down but on we worked until the light of day wasted away. The Mammas all raced back to their children only to find each tiny body drowned. Mas' never said sorry or nothing, he just whipped the Mammas for crying.

Times were hard. Mas' had to feed us and that cost money. Gradually he sold us off. I was one of the last left. But my turn too came to be sold. Once again my future was left hanging in the air. I was again shown to the sea of white faces. My now not-so-fine teeth were put on show and once again my life was bought away. This time to another black man. He took my two arms and looked deep into my eyes.

'Child,' he said kindly, 'child, you are now free from the whip of the white man.'

Then he just turned his back and walked away. I was so shocked I never said thank you or nothing. That man saved my life. If only I could find him ...

Shanty town – San Antonio

Life is by no means easy now but at least I can rule my own life. At least I am not sold or treated like an animal. At least now my life isn't ruled by a whip. People will still push us out of their shops, people still spit at us and throw stones at us. Nevertheless, I am for the time being happy with the little I have and even that is no thanks to Mas' Montgomery and his type.

Writing this down has helped me clear up my past and perhaps will make my future not quite so bleak. Maybe, too, it will make you more grateful for what you've got.

Oil

SABA RAHMANI

Boots on my feet,
gun in my hand,
kill another soldier,
my head in the sand.

Man on a boat,
shoot down a plane.
Want more crude oil,
need more acid rain.

Milk factory bombed,
children are crying.
Treaty and torture,
while soldiers are dying.

Towns like Riyadh,
hit by a Scud.
People's dead bodies,
dust into mud.

Fathers and brothers,
killed in a raid.
No asking questions,
orders obeyed.

Great Britain and France,
good old U.S.A.
have come to fight
and blow Saddam away.

People protest,
in every alley and street.
Man being tortured,
'Cut off his feet!'

My friends and my fathers,
killed in the war.
No need to ask
what it is all for –

Oil

Last Christmas

SARAH RYAN

The solitary photo of Daddy is discretely hidden behind a bottle of French wine. Mother rushes about the kitchen trying to look busy – the more you have to do the less time you have to think, to remember. Keith plays with old toys he has grown out of. I stand and polish already sparkling cutlery. An unspoken agreement not to remember Daddy.

Last year our seemingly enchanting Christmas quickly turned to a nightmare. Daddy drove us to church in our gleaming, new Ford Granada. We stood in the front pew, a complete family, as we sang joyful hymns rejoicing in the birth of Christ. We were a very religious family, united in our love for God and each other. Outside after the service, Daddy and Uncle Brian discussed the brutal murder of two Catholic boys. Daddy shook his head in disgust; he abhorred violence, especially at Christmas. Though we were Protestants, Daddy always judged people by their character and not their religion.

In the bitter cold this year we walked to church. Mother can't drive. The dusty Ford Granada lies dormant in the garage. In spite of Mother's efforts we were late and stumbled into the end pew. Once joyful hymns no longer held any meaning. I stared blankly at the crib as my mind wandered. Aunt Ellen reminded us that she would be over for dinner. She told us a joke we had heard Daddy say once. No one laughed. Keith complained of the cold and we walked home.

Daddy had chased Keith about the house in a cowboy's hat. He jumped on a breathless Keith who shrieked, 'Daddy, Daddy, I'm a good Indian, really I am.' In a gruff voice Daddy replied, 'I got you now, Indian, and I'm gonna tickle you to death.' Mother chatted with Aunt Ellen in the kitchen as Uncle Brian smoked a cigar. I lit the Christmas candles on the diningroom table and called the family in for dinner.

We bustled into the diningroom and sat down. Then, noticing the place cards I had made assigning each person to a special place, we got up and moved. Daddy swopped places with Uncle Brian. Sometimes I think that Daddy would still be alive if I had let Uncle Brian sit in front of the window.

Daddy licked his lips as Mother carried in the delicious turkey. Uncle Brian asked if she had hired someone to cook since he could never remember her ever making anything edible. Everyone laughed at his joke. Then we bowed our heads as Daddy said grace and thanked God for our food, our health and our family. 'Amen.'

Suddenly, from outside – a shot. The shattering of glass, a second shot, then the blood. Everywhere stained with blood. Mother screamed, Keith ran to Daddy and told him to get off the table, 'Where is the blood coming from?' he asked.

Uncle Brian swore, 'Damn I.R.A.', and ran outside as a car swerved down the road. I held Daddy close while Aunt Ellen rang for an ambulance. But he was already dead.

Now as I sit at the diningroom table one year later I bitterly notice one thing which hasn't changed. The war between the Catholics and Protestants, Nationalists and Unionists, rages on. The violence continues. Mother carries in the turkey and Uncle Brian says it looks tasty. Everyone agrees. I stare at the empty seat in front of the window and I notice a single tear trickle down my mother's face. Keith complains that he is not hungry. Aunt Ellen corrects him. Yet no one moves and the feast grows cold. The turkey lies uncarved and the bottle of French wine untouched.

My Doggie
EMMA LONG

I have a little doggie
Sally is her name
she is a little Yorkie
she has a little tail.
I walk her every evening
just before it's dark
whenever I forget to,
she always starts to bark.
Whenever I have troubles
I tell my little friend
she always sits and listens
she makes my heartaches mend.

My Home
CLIODHNA MARTIN

Up in the attic
all dark and damp,
with Jasper's bark —
now and then —
but you really
don't know when.

James's Quest

SEAMUS O'BRIEN

Characters

James
wizard
baron
apple seller
villager
soldier
monsters
black demon
river troll
robot person
the Robot King
the King of the Knights
the Ice King
ice person

Wizard: James, you have been picked to go on a quest to find the six scrolls of Titon.

James: Wizard, why have I been chosen to lead this quest?

Wizard: You are no great warrior, but you are noble and trustworthy. Do you accept the challenge?

James: I accept.

Wizard: Go now and fulfil your quest!

James walks out of the room happy but unsure. After a few days he is not familiar with the surrounding landscape. He sees an apple seller with his load.

James to apple seller: Tell me what world I am in.

Apple seller: This is Endor, and it is ruled by the river troll.

James: The river troll. Tell me where he dwells.

Apple seller: He sits on that tree stump every day at six o'clock.

James: It's six o'clock now!

James walks over to the tree stump and a green troll appears!

James: Troll, do you have the first scroll?

River Troll: I have the required scroll. To get it you must answer this riddle: what has a mouth but never talks?

James: A river!

The troll frowns and hands over the scroll. James thanks him with a snigger! The troll disappears in a cloud of dust.

The wizard appears and tells James he will have to face a black demon in the next world! James enters the next world.

James thinks about having to face a black demon and gets a sick feeling in his stomach but is reassured when he remembers he only has to answer riddles to get the required scrolls. James sees an army approaching.

James to head soldier: Do you know of the black demon?

Head soldier: Yes, I do, but I wouldn't get on his bad side as he can be very nasty!

James: You must tell me where he lives.

Head soldier: He doesn't live anywhere. Here, recite these words as written. If you recite them imperfectly you will be frozen in time!

The soldier hands James a piece of vellum in which the words are written. James recites the words which are: deib reic flimebarneo! *The black demon appears with a ghostly grim look on his face!*

Black demon: Who are you and what do you want?

James: I am James, and I believe you have the second scroll of Titon.

Black demon: Answer this riddle: what has a tongue but doesn't speak?

James: Fire?

A scroll appears, James takes it and moves on. The wizard disappears. James finds himself in a land of fire and brimstone. He finds out the inhabitants are people of fire!

James to villager: Tell me where I will find two fierce monsters.

The villager looks surprised as James is not of fire. James finds out that the two monsters rule the land. He is taken to the monsters as the villager thinks he is an evil spirit!

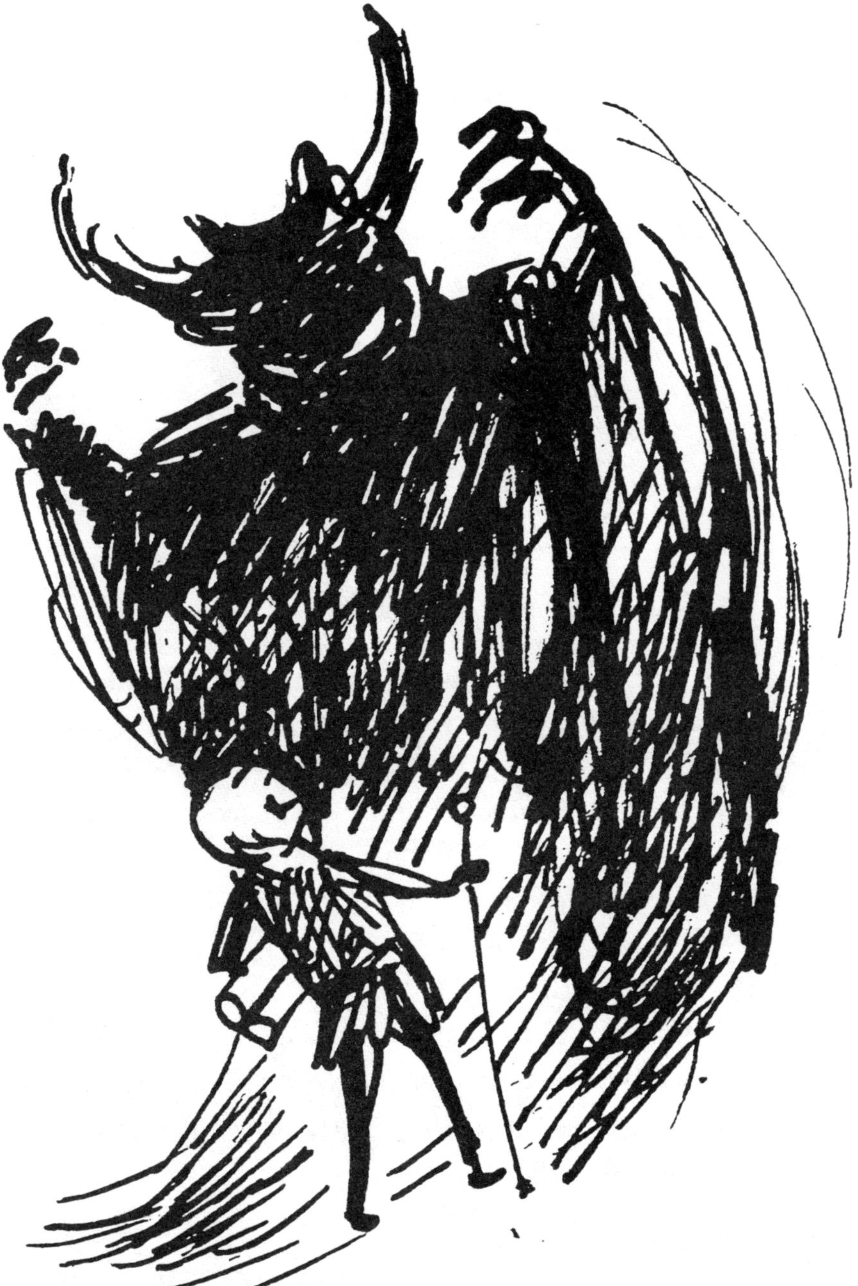

Monster no.1: What do you want in this world and why does your leader want to harm us?

James: I mean you or your kind no harm. I need the third scroll of Titon.

Monster no.2: We have that scroll.

James: Tell me your riddle.

Monster no.1: Here is the riddle: what has a bell but does not ring, but yet its knell makes the angels sing?

James thinks with an unsure look on his face, then finds the answer!

James: A bluebell!

The second monster hands over the scroll. James enters the next world. James finds the next world is ruled by robots! He is amazed to see robot people!

James to robot person: Tell me, where is your ruler?

Robot person: He is in his quarters, but I can take you there myself.

James: Thank you.

The robot clicks his fingers and two flying boards appear. They travel very fast and it does not take them long to reach their destination.

James to Robot King: You have the fourth scroll of Titon.

Robot King: Here is your riddle: what shines in the night but doesn't have its own light?

James thinks about the riddle and after a while finds the answer!

James: The moon!

Robot King: That's the correct answer! Here's your scroll.

James takes the scroll from the Robot King's hand and enters the next world very pleased.

The wizard appears and tells James his destiny is nearly over. He also says if James answers a riddle incorrectly he will be a slave in that world. James finds himself in a world of ice! He sees that the inhabitants are people of ice!

James to ice person: I need to talk to your leader.

Ice person: I will take you to him as he will be interested in seeing a person of flesh and blood!

James is taken to the Ice King.

James to Ice King: King of the ice people, tell me your riddle with which to get the scroll.

Ice King: Here is your riddle: ice and snow can give this to you but it leaves no mark of teeth!

James thinks and finds the answer.

James: That's easy, frostbite.

He hands James the scroll with an icy glare!

James enters a world of knights.

Knight: Who are you and where do you come from?

James: I am James and I come from a world far from here. I have to find the last scroll of Titon.

Knight: Our leader has the scroll.

The soldier calls the baron.

James to baron: Tell me your riddle.

Baron: What to a foolish man's eyes may look like gold but when you get nearer its secret is told?

James: A wheat field.

He hands over the scroll. James's quest is fulfilled. He goes back to his own world. The wizard thanks him and James is made viceroy to the king!

Life on a Farm

ANNA-MARIE HIGGINS

There are many animals on a farm. Some are horses and cows. There are many other animals. There are many different farms. There are fish farms, mixed farms, sheep and cattle farms.

I myself live on a mixed farm.

Farm life is free and easy. The farmer and his children have to be careful with the machinery.

In spring the farmer expects the cows to calve and the sheep to lamb. He ploughs the fields and sows the crops.

First he ploughs the fields and harrows them. He sows the oats and barley with the corn drill. He sows the potatoes with the potato planter. He sows the turnips with the turnip machine. He also sows the fodder beet with the turnip machine.

All of these crops have to be sprayed for pests. He guards his sheep from foxes and dogs that would kill them.

On our way to school we see birds building nests. In late spring the cuckoo comes to Ireland and baby birds are born.

In summer the farmer expects the horses to foal. He is very busy cutting the hay and silage. He also has to save the hay. He sometimes makes round bale silage to avoid polluting rivers and the air. He has to guard his potatoes from the birds and his carrots and cabbage from rabbits and pheasants.

He has to cut and save turf to keep warm.

When he is in the bog he has to watch his children from running too far. He also goes to the seaside for a break.

In autumn the farmer is very busy because he has to cut the corn, dig potatoes, gather carrots and other vegetables.

He has to bring other animals in. He has to ready the sheds for animals and straw.

His wife gathers apples from the apple trees and blackberries for jam.

In autumn the grass changes colour from green to yellow. Leaves fall from trees and become very bare. The country changes, it looks like no one lives there.

In winter, life on the farm can be very hard because no matter whether it's wet, cold, rain or snow, he has to go out to feed his cattle, sheep and all the other animals with grain, nuts, hay or silage.

The farmer's wife and children gather holly and mistletoe. The farmer and his wife leave food for birds. Christmas is a big big break for winter.

Different birds migrate from Ireland to warmer countries.

Other little animals go to sleep for the winter with a store of food. The hedgehog goes to sleep for winter but it does not have a store of food.

This is the way life is worked all through the year.

A Shark Called Bugsy Brown

A L I S O N   M C   C L E L L A N D

Once upon a time there was a shark called Bugsy Brown.

Bugsy Brown went to the top of the water to look at the world and he found three fish lying on the top of the water. He said, 'Mmmm yum-yum. I think they are dead so I can eat them.'

He looked at them. Bugsy Brown did not know that they were only pretending to be dead. You see, the fish were feeling bored so they decided to look for a chase. The fish began to swim as fast as they could with Bugsy Brown right behind them. They headed straight for a cave. Bugsy Brown bashed his head against the cave wall. 'I will get you for that.'

The fish laughed and laughed and laughed.

They had a plan to make Bugsy Brown their friend. They said, 'Please be our friend because when we grow up we will be nearly as big as you.' Nobody likes sharks and Bugsy had no friends, so he thought that he would bring the little fish to his house.

Then he would have great fun with his new friends.

Trees in Winter

RAHMONA HENRY

Winter approached
sneaking up on autumn
trees were frightened
they knew what was about to happen
their children would be torn away
they would be left
standing like skeletons in the wind
arms reaching out
in the wind for help
but nobody would come.

Trees

MIRIAM SWEENEY

Trees are tall and some are small. The bark of some trees is brown. Paper is made from bark.

Some children climb trees.

I like apple trees. The apples from the apple tree are very nice and Mummy makes apple tarts with them. I like picking apples.

There are many names for trees, like banana tree, orange tree, grape tree, plum tree and conker tree.

My friend Claire likes trees too. We are getting a Christmas tree.

Sometimes I think there are too many trees in the park, sometimes the wind knocks them down and that frightens me. I don't like the wind and the trees together in the park.

The Quest of the Sarakai

MARK FOTTRELL

Far away, in distance and time, there is a planet inhabited by ancestors of mankind. It is a world of three suns, each a dim object from which emanates little light but an unbearable heat. The mingled light of the three provides red skies, but over time has also provided a red barren desert. All the ground here is red and cracked. There are dried-up river beds, a few of which have a trickle of water running through them. There are also the remains of once great cities and a once great civilisation, now dust like the plants they lived upon.

As in every species of creature, the fittest have survived. They are now a dwindling tribe of warriors numbering no more than one thousand. They called themselves the Sarakai. The Sarakai believed that a great enemy would come some day and battle would be met upon the Desert of Death. So, the Sarakai trained and prepared for battle, and death.

One of the Sarakai children, a boy called Arabor, desired to become the greatest warrior of his people. His father was renowned for his prowess in handling a sword, and for his great wisdom, which many people sought. Arabor had a twin sister called Irannon, who, like her brother, had the spirit of a warrior inside her. But she had more wisdom than her brother.

It happened that at this time it was nearing Arabor's time of ascension. He would soon become a warrior. Unknown, however, was that Irannon had been trained in the disciplines of a warrior by her father. This was kept a secret though, as women were not permitted to become warriors and training them was frowned upon.

The day of the ascension test arrived. Arabor went with his father to the Circle of Ascension, the most sacred place in all the lands of the Sarakai. From here, it was said, the power that upheld the Sarakai emanated.

All the elders and warriors had gathered. The test was announced. Arabor's quest was to cross the Plains of Silence and enter the Valley of Death Fortress. He then had to claim the Gauntlet of Ascension. He had to do this and return by sunset the next day. Arabor rode off, accompanied by two warriors dressed in black. As they neared the edge of the plains, the warriors turned back. Little did they know that Arabor would not be alone.

Back at the Circle, Arabor and Irannon's mother had arrived. She announced that Irannon was missing and was feared to have followed Arabor her brother. This news disturbed the warriors, who wanted to follow Arabor and Irannon and bring them back. The chief elder stopped them saying, 'Once begun, the test may not be stopped for anything without bringing failure.'

Arabor entered the Plains of Silence. He suddenly had an uncontrollable urge to shout. As soon as he did so, the sound died and nothing could be heard. Suddenly, Arabor felt a cold hand on his shoulder and swiftly he turned, drawing the short sword he always carried. The sight that met him struck him dumb and motionless and the sword fell from his hand.

There stood Irannon, in the raiment of a warrior, carrying a sword by her side and a shield upon her back.

'Irannon,' said Arabor, 'why have you come? There is much danger ahead. You know you are not permitted to attempt the test.'

He bent down and picked up his sword. 'Irannon,' he repeated. 'Irannon, why do you not answer?'

'My brother,' she replied. 'I had to come. It is my destiny to become the first warrioress of the Sarakai.'

'You must go back,' Arabor said again. 'I will not continue.'

'You know the test may only be taken once and failure means disgrace and exile,' Irannon replied.

'If you stop, you will fail. There are many hidden dangers ahead and you may need my help.'

So they carried on together not knowing that hostile eyes were always upon them.

Near sunset on the first day they stopped and made a small fire. When it was dark and they had eaten, Arabor said he would take the first watch, not that he thought there was much to watch for. At about midnight he saw the glint of a sword in the moonlight and at once he drew his sword and went to check it out. Suddenly he was grabbed from behind. He flung the assailant over his shoulder and went to deal a fatal blow, but his sword was met by another. The noise woke Irannon and she drew her sword and went to her brother's aid and the two attacked from either side. Then Arabor dealt a fatal blow which pierced the assailant's rib cage, heart and spine.

The next day a body could be seen in that spot. Gradually over time it decomposed into nothingness. After cleaning their swords the two moved on, fearful of further attacks.

At first light, Arabor and Irannon entered into the Valley of Death Fortress. Far ahead in the distance Death Fortress could be seen veiled by a thin, eerie mist.

They proceeded alongside a dried-up riverbed which had once flowed from the fortress. A sudden sound alerted them to a flock of birds which had been startled. They paid little heed though, as they thought they had disturbed the birds. But as they neared the fortress they were stopped by an arrow which pierced the ground in front of them. Quickly they drew their weapons and Irannon took the shield from her back and held it in front of the two of them. They could see nothing and they turned to the arrow. On it was a message. It read: *Death Fortress is not idly named! Beware!'*

Soon afterwards they arrived at the fortress. They moved cautiously. They entered by a large window and headed for the inner chamber. Cautiously, they moved forward, swords drawn, checking for traps.

Suddenly, Arabor stepped on a trap-door which had rotted. As the ground went from under him, he shouted to Irannon, who immediately came to his aid. Arabor clutched onto the floor but was steadily losing his grip. Just as his hands slipped, an arm shot out and grabbed his wrist. He looked up and saw the silhouette of Irannon. She managed to pull him out and they carried on.

Minutes later they reached the inner chamber. Carefully they opened the doors and moved into the chamber silently. There at the centre stood a pedestal upon which was set the Gauntlet of Ascension, a diamond-encrusted, solid gold glove, which sparkled in the dim sunlight. Arabor and Irannon moved slowly forward, but when they came to the pedestal neither one of them was able to move or speak. They were both struck with awe. This quickly wore off though and they took the gauntlet and ran. In the corridor leading to the exit, they were stopped once again.

This time it was by a ferocious-looking band of men. These were the exiles, the ones who had failed, and they were out to gain revenge. They it was who had brought the name Death Fortress. Now they blocked all the escape routes. Arabor and Irannon stood back-to-back and drew their weapons. The exiles drew closer. Steel met steel. Arabor and Irannon hacked their way through. Eventually, after much bloodshed, they broke out and ran from the fortress. They were followed for a while, but as they left the valley, the chase was stopped.

They continued on until they were safe. It was only then they noticed that they were both injured. Irannon's leg was badly cut, as were Arabor's leg and sword arm. They did their best to tend their wounds, and carried on.

They hurriedly crossed the plains and soon after arrived back at the Circle of Ascension. They were met by the warriors who treated their wounds. As they ate, Arabor and Irannon told their story.

Just before sunset, they went before the chief elder and together they presented the Gauntlet of Ascension to him. He accepted it and said that never had so much been overcome by two so young.

To Arabor was given the title of warrior. He also received a long broadsword, the hilt of which was gold, and diamond-encrusted. The blade was inscribed with many magic runes.

Irannon was made warrioress and received the twin of Arabor's sword. She was the first warrioress of the Sarakai. Her destiny was fulfilled.

An Tuaisceart

NIALL MAC INNÉIRÍ

Phléasc buama sa Tuaisceart aréir.
Saol eile imithe gan ghreann!
Cé hiad na daoine uafásacha seo,
Atá ag scriosadh ár ndomhain?

Sceimhlitheoirí agus saighdiúirí,
Gach rud i mbaol!
Tarlaíonn sé sa dorchadas,
Níl meas acu ar an SAOL!

Cathain a bheidh deireadh leis an marú seo,
Go mbeidh daoine mar chairde le grá?
Gur féidir leo siúl gan eagla ar bith,
Cathain a thiocfaidh an Lá?

Don't Worry, Be Yourself

R U T H F I N N E R A N

It's really depressing. No one understands me, especially not my parents and teachers. My parents say, 'It's a phase you're going through, my lad.' My teachers all simply say, 'Has no concentration. Needs help.'

I'm tired of being only Brian Tully. I mean, how boring can you get? None of the girls are interested in me. I'm not really surprised. I mean, I don't play football or rugby like all the dudes in my class do. Yea, I'm just Brian. Boring Brian.

I'd like to get away from it all. Maybe if I took up sport ...

Reporter 1
'Another gold for Ireland's all fabulous Bold Brian. Yes, he's crossed that finishing line 7.2 seconds after leaving his starting point. Nothing can hold this man back now!'

Reporter 2
'The crowds in Barcelona, Olympics 1992, are going wild! Brian the Bullet has beaten the world record in the men's 100 metres by 0.5 of a second. He's a true legend in athletics. His like won't be seen again!'

'Brian, Brian Tully, get back here this instant!'

It was old pimple-nose himself, Mr Gallaher, the headmaster. 'Where do you think you're going? You know the rules about running in the corridors!'

'Oh yea. Sorry, sir, but I was well, em, late for class. Yea, that's right. Late for class.' I stuttered back to him.

'Just to inform you,' God himself bellowed back, 'it's just gone four o'clock. School is over for today.'

I glared at my watch. How could I have been so stupid? Why didn't I say my dog was dying or something? But being late for class at four o'clock! I slowly looked up. There was silence for what seemed like an hour.

'You're on detention. Well, go on then. Down to room 12,' he said sternly. He then swung round and left me standing in the long echoing corridor with only the lockers and litter to keep me company.

Well, as you can guess, I was quite ready to blow a fuse. On detention for running down a corridor. I didn't even bump into him. I'd, I'd ...

'7, 8, 9, 10. He's out! Terrible Tully has cleaned up that fight in only the second round. This man shows no mercy. Even his heaviest opponents he wipes out without batting an eyelid!

'The screams of the hysterical women are deafening as Terrible Tully parades around the boxing ring. Kisses and flowers are being thrown at him from all sides now. Then the moment of truth arrives. Tully is presented, by a

beautiful blonde, with the World Heavyweight Boxing Championship Cup for 1992. He raises it over his head with delight ...'

'Ouch!' I cried as my Irish book tumbled down onto my head. It was only then that I noticed I was holding my open school bag aloft in the air above my head.

Back to reality I suppose. I kicked my schoolbag down the corridor for a while. My head was buzzing with thoughts. My main one was, of course, Angeline Gould. A gorgeous girl with auburn hair and blue eyes who sits in front of me in class. I spend my days dreaming about how someday she may actually notice that I'm alive. I always embarrass myself just when she looks my way. She must think that I'm a right plonker. How I long for the day when she says: I've been blind, Brian. I don't see how I never noticed your good looks and charm. Please forgive me!

Then she'll flicker her eyelashes and gaze into the depths of my eyes ...

Aw Brian, cop on, would ya? She'll never be interested in you. You'll find someone. I often have to reassure myself about these things. I continued down the corridor nearer to room 12. Nearer ...

'He's nearing the goal. Tackled from all sides by the Italian full-backs. Such skill, such control! He shoots, it's a bullet into the corner of the net. It's brave, bold Brian Tully yet again! Yes, there's the whistle! Tully has scored

the winning goal for Ireland in this World Cup Championship here in Germany! He was, only last year, a young school lad with undiscovered talents and this year he's got more goals than any other player in this championship! We have news which has just come in – what's this? Tully is to be married to the most beautiful Angeline Gould next May! They have just announced their engagement. What a fine couple they'll make!'

The door of room 12 swung open. Out marched Miss Loyde, looking like a pickled onion. She had her usual white blouse, grey jacket and straight skirt on her. I often thought that it's a straitjacket that she should have on her and not a straight skirt!

She looked down her nose at me. I hated that. It always made me feel like trash.

'Well, boy, are you going to stay out here for the day?' she rudely inquired.

'No, miss. I was just going …' I replied.

'You were just nothing. Get inside and don't let there be a word from you!' she barked.

I felt as though I was walking through 'no-man's land' in World War II, I could almost hear the engines of the bomber planes zooming over my head. Shots sounded in the distance and then … a distant light flickered …'

I rubbed my weary eyes to see if I could be mistaken, but no! There in front of my very own eyes was Angeline Gould – the girl of my dreams!

I brushed straight past all the 'hards' of the school (who think they're really cool and tough), who grasped their flick-knives in their over-grown mouldy hands.

The only desk free was beside Angeline. That didn't bother me! I was just about to sit down when one of the 'hards' pulled the chair from under me. I fell straight down under my desk, hitting my chin on the way. There I went again, making a fool out of myself in front of Angeline.

I pulled myself together and settled my chair to its original position. I then got seated and took out my books. The laughing had settled down a bit but the redness of my swollen face had not.

Miss Loyde stormed down to the back of the classroom and dragged the fellow who caused the accident out of the room by his pony tail.

As soon as they'd gone, chaos broke loose in the classroom. Suddenly a bloke with earrings and a shaved head came on strong with Angeline. Angeline tried to ignore him. It was obvious that he was annoying her.

I swung around and leapt out of my seat. I was taking no more nonsense. I was tired of being told what to do and about how stupid and boring I was. I knew all that now, so it was time to do something about it.

I clenched my fist and hurled it in the 'hard's' direction. It almost sent him flying! I didn't care about him or the pain that was caused to my hand. All I cared about was the look of gratitude on Angeline's face. She was beaming from ear to ear. Now that I'd finally faced up to myself I didn't know what to do! I sort of *panicked*!

Hearing all the commotion, Miss Loyde barged in. She was frowning so hard that she looked like a bulldog. She roared: 'What happened here? Who did this? Tell me NOW!'

Angeline stood up, put her arm around me, sat me down and said, 'He's all right, miss. Everything's going to be all right now.'

Then the bell went and everyone bulldozed out of the room. They woke Charlie, the fellow I knocked out, and ran out of the room. Miss Loyde chased after him to find out the full story.

Angeline and I walked home slowly that evening. I never worried about the future from then on. I just faced up to it! So now I say, 'Don't worry, be yourself and of course – be happy!'

The Friendly Giant

E M E R D E L A N E Y

Once upon a time there was a huge, high hill. On the top of this hill there was a castle. In the castle lived a prince who had a spell on him. The prince's name was Eric and the spell was that he had to be a giant. The spell could only be broken if a beautiful princess would fall in love with him. A witch had put on this bad spell.

Now one day a princess came. She was actually the most beautiful girl in the world. As soon as Eric told her that he was really a prince she said, 'I will help you. I will fall in love with you.'

The witch heard and was furious. She said, 'I know what I'll do. I'll make myself like the princess. Then Eric will think that I am his precious princess and my spell will last.'

So her servants made the witch beautiful. Eric did mistake her for his princess. Also, the princess's father heard about his daughter being in love with the giant. He did not know that the giant was friendly. He said to his daughter, 'You know you must not be in love with bad people.' But the princess still loved the prince.

Then the witch turned the princess into a flower, and she herself was still a beautiful girl. But Eric said, 'That flower is more beautiful than this girl.'

The spell was broken on both of them. Then Eric and the princess were married and lived happily ever after.

Avenging the Grape

GERALDINE HAYES

'I've got it!' yelled the Professor, jumping up wildly, shaggy beard floating round his wizened face.

'Got what, darling?' asked his wife calmly from the kitchen.

'The potion,' said the Professor, as if she should know.

'What potion?' asked his wife, patiently as usual. She was used to the Professor's moods of wild delight or gloomy discouragement, and rarely took any notice anymore.

'The potion to enlarge species of fruit and vegetables!' yelled the Professor impatiently, in direct contrast to his level-headed wife.

'Oh good!' beamed his wife. 'No more peeling mountains of potatoes! I am glad!'

The Professor looked at his wife, shaking his head as if giving her up as a lost cause. 'Look, Mildred,' he tried to explain, 'with my new potion, we could feed millions of starving people with just one carrot each per week!'

'Even better!' she beamed. 'Oh, and my name's Susan. Mildred is your mother.'

The Professor shook his head, as if trying to figure out the difference.

The fruit in the basket listened to all this with growing apprehension. Because they might be heard, they could not speak and so they communicated their feelings by rolling their eyes and shuddering violently.

'I think I'll try it out now,' they heard the Professor boom, followed by loud footsteps towards the fruit basket. Then they all got the full beauty of the Professor's small, wrinkled and bearded face peering into the basket. One of the young grapelettes was so scared it let out a squeal, and was severely pinched by its playmates. Luckily, the Professor didn't hear.

He picked out a large grape, which

was, unknown to him, the Commanding Grape. The grape's wife clung to her husband momentarily, but to no avail. The Professor took the small bottle of green liquid from the dresser and removed the cap. The fear on the grape's face was terrible to look at. His wife quickly looked away as the Professor cut him open. All the young fruitlettes looked on, fascinated, as he poured a drop of the green stuff into the grape. He was then placed on the table, and watched closely by the Professor.

Slowly the grape began to grow. He grew and grew, until he was the size of the table. He grew until he touched the ceiling. The fruit in the basket watched from the safety of the dresser as the unfortunate grape expanded until – BANG! The grape exploded, drenching everything in grape juice. By now the grape's wife was hysterical, and she wasn't the only one. The Professor's wife was going crazy too, yelling and screaming at him in a rage.

'Look at the mess, you stupid wally!' she screamed. 'Well, you made it, you can mop it up!'

'Calm down,' he said distantly, trying to figure out what had gone wrong.

'Calm down he says! *Calm down!*' she laughed, and then became angry again. 'That's a good one, coming from you!' With that, she swept out of the room, saying, 'There are some dry cloths in the press. Wash them out when you're finished.' The Professor sighed as he began mopping up the mess.

All was dark that night when the fruit considered it safe to come out of the basket. The shock had worn off by now, and was replaced by anger. Everyone was yelling at once. A Commanding Apple hoisted himself up to the top of the basket, and cleared his throat. The noise gradually disappeared, as the fruit looked expectantly at Captain Apple.

'Ladies, gentlefruit, and fruitlettes,' he began, 'you all know, of course, of the sudden and violent death of our dear friend and helper, Captain Grape.' At that, the bereaved wife began to wail again, but was quickly hushed.

'Get on with it,' yelled a banana, and a group of defiant plums began to chant, 'We want action! We want action!'

'Will someone please shut those berks up!' said Captain Apple. The plums were quickly gagged, and the chanting subsided.

The meeting went on, suggestions flying to and fro. 'Let's kill him!' or 'We could always give him some of his own potion.' After this statement, an awed silence descended on the room. The tiny strawberry who had suggested this was regarded with respect and awe. She looked very pleased with herself. The plums quickly ungagged themselves, and began to yell, 'Make him explode! Make him explode!' At that, the bereaved wife began to cry again.

'My heart can't stand the strain,' murmured Captain Apple, mopping his brow.

But the plums, seeing the glares from the other fruit, replaced their gags and made themselves as small as possible. Two gooseberries made a collection of handkerchiefs and stuffed them into the mouth of the wailing grape. Soon all was silent again.

'Right, then,' said Captain Apple. 'Let's make our plans.'

Next morning, the Professor's wife made him a cup of tea, and was about to bring it up to him when the doorbell rang. She put down the tea, went to the door, and opened it to find a bag of rather grubby oranges in the porch.

'Now I wonder who can have sent these?' she said.

Meanwhile, the tallest bananas had carried the bottle of potion to the Professor's cup of tea, and had just unscrewed the cap when they heard his wife returning. They quickly emptied the whole bottle into the tea, and dropped down onto the counter.

Susan, or Mildred, took no notice of them or the bottle. She took the cup and went upstairs. As soon as she had gone, the fruit all evacuated to the garden where they watched expectantly. Soon they heard screaming, and the Professor's wife legged it into the garden and over the back wall (which was, as a matter of interest, six feet high). Then the Professor's enormous foot came crashing through the kitchen wall. Suddenly, his head appeared through the roof of the house. Almost immediately there was a huge explosion, and the Professor was nothing but an almighty mess.

The Professor's wife was never heard of again, and as for the fruit, they became outfruits and grew wild!

Am Taistil

DARA DE BÚRCA

Lá amháin nuair a bhí mé ag imirt le mo ríomhaire tháinig mo chara trasna go dtí mo theach. Bhíodh sé i gcónaí ag pleidhcíocht le rudaí leictreacha ar nós raidió briste, teilifís briste, soilse, cnaipí ón mballa agus bataire mór ó charr! An uair seo bhí rud an-aisteach ina láimh aige agus crios le cnaipe mór dearg air. Dúirt sé liom go raibh sé in ann taisteal tríd an am leis an rud aisteach seo. Ar dtús phléasc mé amach ag gáire ag ceapadh gur cleas a bhí ann ach ansin tar éis tamaill thuig mé nach raibh sé ag magadh fúm.

Dúirt se liom go gcaithfí é a chur isteach i ríomhaire. 'Ceart go leor,' a dúirt mé tar éis nóiméad nó dhó ag smaoineamh faoi. Thosaíomar ar an rud a chur isteach sa ríomhaire agus nuair a bhí sé sin déanta againn chuir mé an ríomhaire ar siúl. Scríobh mo chara dáta ar an ríomhaire agus bhrúigh sé an cnaipe dearg. 'Slán,' a dúirt sé agus d'imigh sé as radharc na súl.

Ansin d'fhéach mé ar mhonatóir an ríomhaire. Thaispeáin sé mo chara ag dul trí am! Nuair a stop sé bhí sé sa bhliain a bhí sé tar éis a scríobh leis an ríomhaire – 1942 – i lár an dara chogadh domhanda!

Bhí sé ar tí a mharaithe ach nuair a chonaic sé é seo bhuail sé an cnaipe dearg ar an bpointe.

'Bhí sé sin go hiontach,' ar seisean.

Ansin bhain mise triail as. Scríobh mé isteach an bhliain 1169 – an bhliain a tháinig na Normannaigh go hÉirinn. Thóg mé an crios ó mo chara agus bhrúigh mé an cnaipe dearg. Tar éis cúpla soicind bhí mé ann, 1169 i gCuan an Bhainbh i gCo. Loch Garman.

D'fhéach mé amach ar an bhfarraige agus cinnte go leor bhí na báid Normannacha ag teacht ar an ionsaí. Rith mé síos an sráidbhaile agus dúirt mé leis na daoine go raibh na Normannaigh ag teacht. Thóg na saighdiúirí amach a gcuid arm. Anois bhí siad réidh dóibh. Chuaigh siad síos go dtí an cuan agus chuaigh siad i bhfolach. Ag an am céanna bhí mná, sagairt agus páistí ag rith suas go dtí an Tiarna chun áit a fháil chun go mbeadh cosaint éigin acu ó na strainséirí seo a bhí ag teacht. Ní raibh aon duine fágtha sa bhaile. Chuaigh mé síos go dtí an cuan chun féachaint ar an arm. Bhí mo chuid oibre déanta agam – bhí an t-arm réidh agus bhí na sibhialtaigh slán sábháilte. Bhrúigh mé an cnaipe dearg chun dul ar ais abhaile ach níor oibrigh sé! Bhí mé i bhfostú i 1169.

Bhí mé i dtrioblóid cheart anois. Bhí na Normannaigh ag teacht agus mharófaí mé mura mbeadh áit agam chun dul i bhfolach. Bhain mé triail as an gcnaipe arís is arís eile, ach níor oibrigh sé. Bhí banda leaisteach mór tiubh agam i mo phóca agus rinne mé crann tabhaill as.

Bhí mé réidh chun troda. Phioc mé suas cúpla cloch ghéar agus shiúil mé síos go dtí an cuan. Chuaigh mé i bhfolach leis na saighdiúirí eile. Tháinig na Normannaigh i dtír. Chomh luath is a chuir an saighdiúir Normannach deireanach cos ar an trá bhí troid uafásach ann. Bhuail mé cúpla saighdiúir le mo chrann tabhaill agus maraíodh iad. Chuaigh an troid ar aghaidh ar feadh timpeall trí nó ceithre huaire an chloig. Bhí an bua ag na Normannaigh agus maraíodh a lán de na hÉireannaigh.

Nuair a bhí na Normannaigh imithe chuaigh mé suas go dtí teach an Tiarna agus nuair a shroich mé é ghabh na daoine buíochas liom as ucht an rabhadh a thabhairt. Bhí béile mór ann. Rinne mé dearmad glan ar 1991. Nuair a bhí an béile thart thosaigh ceoltóir ag seinm ceoil.

Ansin a chuimhnigh mé ar 1991. Bhrúigh mé an cnaipe dearg agus an uair seo d'oibrigh sé. Nuair a chuaigh mé abhaile bhí mé réidh chun mo chara a mharú agus dúirt mé leis go gcaithfí an rud seo a thógáil as a chéile agus go raibh sé ró-dhainséarach. D'aontaigh sé liom agus thógamar as a chéile é. Nuair a bhí sé go léir tógtha as a chéile againn dúirt mo chara, 'Ar ais go dtí an bord tarraingte.'

'Sin é an saol,' arsa mise leis.

The Crab

GILLIAN MC CUSKER

*Crimson am I
running to the shore
always ready to nip
back home before
the tide comes in.*

The Duck

GILLIAN MC CUSKER

Down we are a-dabbling
usually catch a fish.
Caught one yesterday.
Kipper – amazing was it.

The Snail

ISOBEL ABBOTT

*The slimy slitherer,
slowly slid, then stopped.
With no sounds of snoring,
it slept, silently, in the summer sun.*

Saol Mogwa

MIRIAM NIC ARTÚIR

Mogwa is ainm dom. Táim í mo chónaí sa bhforaois bháistí is mó ar domhan sa Brasaíl i Meiriceá Theas. Ithim plandaí cosúil le ionaim, piobair, casabhach agus faighneoga ócra. Uaireanta maraíonn fir na treibhe ainmhithe le haghaidh bia. An caitheamh aimsire is fearr liom ná iascaireacht. Rinne mo Dhaidí slat iascaigh dom agus tá curach beag agam déanta as adhmad. Bím ag seoladh síos cuid den Amasóin ag iascaireacht cúpla uair gach lá.

Nuair a mharaítear ainmhithe baintear an craiceann díobh agus déantar éadaí astu. Déanann na mná agus na cailíní na héadaí. Táimse ag iarraidh a bheith cosúil le m'athair mar is iascaire iontach agus ceannaire na treibhe é freisin agus ba mhaith liomsa a bheith i mo cheannaire chomh maith leis.

Is áit álainn é foraois bháistí na Brasaíle i Meiriceá Theas. Tá mé i mo chónaí i réiteach beag sa bhforaois. Tá ainmhithe fiáine agus éin ina gcónaí san áit seo freisin: an crogall a bhíonn ag snámh san Amasóin, an Anacanda, is í sin an nathair is faide ar domhan, agus ar ndóigh, na muiscítí a chuireann cealg uafásach ionat. Tá féileacáin sa bhforaois chomh mór le héan. Is féidir le cúpla beach do chuid gruaige a ithe. Tá iasc san Amasóin, pioráine a thugtar air, agus má tá timpeall céad díobh san uisce ag an am céanna is féidir leo fear a ithe. Tá damhán alla an-mhór sa bhforaois – an tarantúla a thugtar air. Má chloiseann tú torann ard ó cheann de na crainn gach seans gurb é an glafaire nó an 'howler' dearg atá ag déanamh an torainn. Na héin is fearr liom sa bhforaois bháistí ná an cocatú agus an phearóid. Is éan bán é an cocatú le cleití buí ar bharr a chinn. Bíonn a lán dathanna ar chleití na pearóide agus má thraenálann tú í bíonn sí in ann caint.

Uaireanta bíonn cruinniú againn faoi na rudaí atá ag tarlú sa saol. Ag an gcruinniú deireannach seo mar a bhí. Shuigh an treibh go léir timpeall na tine. Labhair m'athair. Bhí rud tábhachtach le rá aige. Seo mar a dúirt sé. 'Tá rudaí uafásacha ag tarlú don fhoraois. Tá fir gheala ag teacht agus ag leagan síos na gcrann. Nuair a leagtar síos crainn ní fhásann na crainn sin arís. Úsáidtear an talamh mar thalamh feirmeoireachta. Mura stopann na daoine geala de bheith ag gearradh síos na gcrann, ní bheidh foraois bháistí ann níos mó. Ní bheidh aon áit chónaithe againn. Céard a dhéanfaimid?'

Rain

PETER KILLIAN

Rain,
bubbles flying
trickling down
splashing on the ground
clouds
black bubbles
floating black sheep
soft.
Birds go home
drooping trees
rivers swell
streets
nearly empty
lots of traffic jams
puddles everywhere.

The Tale of a Goblin

RUTH MAC NAMARA

There once was a goblin inside a wee girl,
And around her wee hearty the goblin did curl,
He shut out the goodness and shut in the bad,
And the poor evil girly made everyone sad.

She used to be kindly and honest and good,
She used to be friendly as ever she could,
But now she was naughty and harsh to her mum
Who was baffled at what a young witch she'd become.

Her teachers were angry, her friends were upset,
For the goblin had caught her inside his cruel net,
Her heart got much harder, her manners got worse,
Till at last her mum took her to Hannah, the nurse.

The nurse took her heartbeat and said with a frown,
'A naughty wee goblin has got this lass down.
She must take this medicine, one spoon every day
So that into her wee heart some kindness will stray.'

The poor little girly recovered, it's true,
(It's a wonder what modern young nurses can do!)
The goblin his days on an old star must spend,
And his mischievous tricks have now come to an end.

Oceania, Flower of the Deep

UNA HARNETT

Far out to sea on the bed of the ocean, beyond the point which no reckless divers could swim, so deep the civilisation of the Merfolk could not even be imagined – on the sandy bed of the ocean sat Oceania, a princess of beauty. Oceania was unusual. She had eyes the colour of the night and her dark hair was embedded with beautiful sea flowers and her skin a soft coral. But for this her family disowned her, because the other mermaids had crystal clear blue eyes and hair as fair as a shaft of sunlight streaming onto the bed of the ocean. Oceania was considered ugly and her name a bitter sound to every mermaid's ear.

She had lived with this for twelve years now and was still wondering why her family would deliberately avoid her, and other Merfolk would swim far from her whenever she was near. Although she knew she was different in appearance, Oceania thought this did not matter as long as you were kind, gentle and loving. She was right but still her family and the Merfolk feared her strange looks. As far as they were concerned she was ugly and that was the only thing that mattered under the sea.

Her favourite days were those spent with an old seahorse by the name of Maralgae, an old and wise creature of the sea who told her of life above the depths of the ocean and tales of her ancestors. The thing she loved most of all was to break the barrier of the sea and then dive again and swim towards the shore, keeping submerged at all times. Oceania would listen to humans, young and old, telling of the weather and other such things, exchanging banter, smiling and laughing – something Oceania had not experienced with fellow Merfolk.

But something caught her attention one crisp autumn morning. Two middle-aged men were talking about a possible earthquake and saying that there would be a disturbance in the water, and that the majority of fish in this area would be crushed and swallowed up by the earthquake.

She had to do something – but what? Oceania realised the tragedy that would befall the Merfolk and all the inhabitants of the sea. She would have to inform Maralgae and spread the word! With one graceful dive Oceania glided through the schools of fish, avoiding darkened sea-caves which could be dangerous because of their unknown length. She finally arrived at Maralgae's cove, which was cocooned with seaweed and other strange plants. The old seahorse noticed the worried expression in her dark eyes when she told him of the earthquake. Maralgae knew this was not an old whale's tale, but the truth.

Accompanied by Oceania, he brought this tragic news to the attention of the Merfolk. Maralgae was respected and had a noble name among the Merfolk because of his great knowledge. Maralgae happened to know of a series of caves quite a distance from Merville, where they would be safe until the earthquake had stopped. The Merfolk began to make preparations for their journey and to gather up their belongings. When everyone was ready they began their trek. After a long and arduous journey, they reached their destination. The caves were dark and eerie, but would keep them safe.

Then there was a cry from a young mother, screaming that Seary, her daughter, was not with her. A search began among the Merfolk, but she was not with anyone. She must be somewhere along the seatrail or even still in Merville! What a tragedy! Some Merman or Mermaid would have to return to find Seary, because the earthquake was close at hand. But nobody offered to help and the poor mother was terribly distressed. Oceania slipped quietly away.

Gliding through the algae and schools of fish, Oceania eventually reached Merville. She heard a pitiful cry coming from under a large rock. It sounded like a child. There, trapped under the rock, lay Seary, crying.

When she saw Oceania she stopped, but seemed a little afraid. With all her might Oceania managed to move the boulder and Seary swam out from under it. Then Oceania swept her up into her arms and told her not to be afraid, she would take her back to her mother. Oceania swam swiftly away from Merville as she felt a sudden tremor. She had to act fast.

Now they were nearing the caves. Oceania grew weary from carrying the sleeping child in her arms. She was greeted with a cheer and much applause as she gave Seary to her tearful mother. Celebrations soon took place for the courageous Mermaid who had risked her life to save a child. Oceania was awarded a golden oyster for bravery and she was honoured wherever she went. She forgave the Merfolk for being unkind to her and she became a pearl in everyone's heart.

Peig Sayers

KATHLEEN TREACY

Sitting in double Irish, I'm often inclined to ask myself, considering there isn't much else to do, why in the honour of all that is sane am I here? Do I really need to know all this? If so, for what reasons? And finally, yet most importantly, what does Peig Sayers have to do with anything in this non-Gaelic speaking world that's sensible?

Peig, dear, dear Peig, if you are up there, relieve us please of our great and terrible burden. O.K., so to give Peig some credit, she may be considered an important part of our culture and heritage but ... All of this happened over one hundred years ago. What bearing does she have on reality now? Do we really need to know who her brother Seán married, how he got his nickname 'Pounder', or why Peig went into service at thirteen?

Mná na hÉireann, what a prime example Peig is. Well-distinguished, well-educated, a perfect career woman. Her whole life revolved around cleaning up after milking the one cow she possessed. Just imagine how thankful and lucky we'd all be if Tomás Ó Brosnacháin and his wife, Peig The First, had decided not to continue their child-bearing efforts. One less would certainly not have made a difference – they had ten others.

If I, plus ten thousand other school-goers had been around in the days of Peig and the Great Blasket, and had known she was writing or even had intentions of writing her memoirs, then I'm too polite to say what I would have done. When the Department of Education and the minister eventually decide that Peig has served her country whole-heartedly, then I can assure you that a rousing cheer will go up throughout the country as pupils, past and present, relieve their tensions while Peig prepares to lay down her arms and die in glory.

Some glory, being absolutely detested by her native nation, apart from the minority of dedicated Irish speakers, that is.

ALICE HAMILTON

My Brother

I have a brother,
and I don't want another,
if you had a brother,
you would see why.
I would cry and cry and cry
and I would also hit the sky.

The Ship

There was a ship that sunk
because the captain was drunk
the sailors went too
deep down in the blue,
and that was the end of the crew.

A Gruesome Discovery

PETER DURKAN

Ever since I could remember I have been very interested in nature, especially wildlife. I would often spend hours just watching the birds flitting around our back garden. I have read numerous books about bird life and plant life. I probably got my love of nature from my Grandad, who lived on a small farm in the country.

Over the years Grandad had acquired a great store of knowledge about many aspects of the natural world around us and especially the area surrounding his farm. This probably is the main reason why I got such great pleasure in visiting him. It was on one such occasion that I learned the greatest lesson of my life, to respect life in the wild.

My Grandad, because of his love of bird life, used to breed pheasants and was very proud of them. For this purpose he always kept a number of hen pheasants and about two prize cocks.

As I arrived at my Grandad's house that evening in early spring, the snow had just began to spiral down from the ever-darkening sky. It must have snowed all night because when I awoke the next morning the whole countryside was enveloped in a thick mantle of snow – it was a winter wonderland. The snow lay everywhere, on the wall, in the fields, on the fences, and it clung like a white moss to the posts. I was absolutely delighted and fascinated by the way it glittered and glistened in the frosty air of the early spring morning.

As I walked down the stairs I heard a commotion in the kitchen. Later I discovered that one of Grandad's prize cocks and two of his hens were missing. I ran out to examine the pen more closely and there behind it were tracks heading towards the woods. I ran in and told Grandad. When he examined them he discovered that they were fox's tracks. 'Come on,' he said in an anxious tone. 'We have a job to do.' With a cap on his head, a gun on his arm, the dog and me by his side, we set off in pursuit.

The silence of the forest was broken by the occasional cracking of twigs as we followed the tracks deep into the woods. Suddenly the dog started to bark excitedly and a streak of red flashed by. As fast as his legs could carry him the dog followed. I could not keep up with him for long and I wondered where Grandad had got to. At that very moment two shots rang out and shattered the silence and peace of the forest. Quickly I ran in the direction of the shots. As I reached the clearing I saw Grandad standing over the fox. He lay sprawled on the snow and as his life's blood flowed away, the circle of blood turned the fluffy white snow all around him to a bright red colour. I saw a gleam of satisfaction in Grandad's eye. But I was not so sure. This seemed a gory sight to me.

However, Grandad took the fox by the tail and we trudged home through the thick snow with the fox in tow.

As we entered the farmyard Grandad held up the fox triumphantly for all to see. He was elated.

It was about a week later, as I was taking a walk by the quarry at the back of my Grandad's house, that I heard what I thought was a dog's whine behind a bush. I looked, and what did I see but three fox cubs. They were so thin you could see their ribs. When I investigated closer I found that there was a fourth but he was dead. I was puzzled. Why hadn't their mother fed them? Then a sudden realisation dawned on me. The fox we had killed was the mother of these cubs. As I approached them the startled cubs staggered away to the safety of the undergrowth. I picked up the dead one; he was so small and so thin I quickly hid him under a bush and walked slowly back to the house in shocked silence.

When I got home, I didn't talk very much to anyone and I didn't even watch the television. I went to bed early that night. I felt I had blood on my hands.

An Cúl

A O I F E   N Í   G H L I A S Á I N

Mise ag stánadh ar an ngléas ciorclach,
Mise an chathéide.
Ag cosaint le crógacht,
Teannas i m'aghaidh
Cumhacht i mo lámha –
Ach – mise an targaid.

An liathróid ag eitilt,
Ag teacht níos gaire,
Is mise ag fanacht.

Léim mé le neart
Mo lámha sínte amach agam
Ach, gan toradh –

Mo chroí – briste,
Deora i mo shúile
Náire an domhain orm
Is mo bhród ina smidiríní.

I Believe

NEAL BROPHY

I believe my room's clean,
even when my Mum does scream,
'Pick up those men, look at those rocks,
Oh my God, smell those socks.'

'But Mum, it's really clean,' I said.
'What's that smell – it's something dead.'
'There's nothing here, I've had a look –
just this old sandwich in my book.'

An Dara Seans

AOIFE NÍ GHLIASÁIN

Bhí Seán de Búrca cúig bliana déag d'aois agus bhí sé sa tríú bliain. Bhí sé an-ard, scafánta, an-dathúil agus bhí gruaig ghearr fhionn air. Bhí súile gorma áille aige. Bhí sé ábalta gach rud a dhéanamh – sin a cheap gach aon duine faoi, ar aon nós.

Bhí a lán cairde aige ach bhí cara speisialta amháin aige, Pól. Bhí Pól ard agus tanaí agus bhí spéaclaí aige. Ní raibh sé dathúil ach bhí sé an-chineálta, an-fhlaithiúil, an-chothrom agus foighneach. Bhí suim ag an mbeirt acu sa pheil agus bhí siad ar an fhoireann chéanna.

Ar an Satharn bhuail Seán le Pól tar éis an chluiche agus shiúil siad abhaile lena chéile. Ar an mbealach dóibh chonaic siad Máire agus a cara Niamh.

'Seo chugainn é! Seo é! Tá sé an-álainn! Is aoibhinn liom é!' arsa Máire.

'Bí ciúin! Nó cloisfidh sé tú ag caint!' arsa Niamh.

Ansin chuaigh na cailíní trasna an bhóthair agus thosaigh Máire ag caint le Seán.

'Dia duit, a Sheáin,' arsa Máire.

'Dia is Muire duit, a Mháire,' arsa Seán.

'An mbeidh tú ag dul cois farraige amárach?' arsa Máire leis.

'Beidh,' arsa sé.

'B'fhéidir go bhfeicfinn ann tú nó b'fhéidir go mbuailfinn leat agus go rachaimis lena chéile!'

'Sin plean maith! Buail liom ar a haon a chlog amárach anseo,' arsa Seán. Léim croí Mháire le háthas agus bhí sí an-sásta léi féin.

Bhí an lá go hálainn agus bhí an ghrian ag scoilteadh na gcloch. Bhuail Máire le Seán agus chuaigh siad cois farraige. Bhí lá iontach acu ar an trá agus tráthnóna deas ina dhiaidh sin.

Tar éis scoile, ar an Luan, bhuail Máire le Seán agus shiúil siad abhaile lena chéile. Shochraigh siad siúl amach lena chéile agus chuaigh siad go dtí an dioscó ar an Satharn.

Ar an gCeádaoin chuala Máire cnag ar an doras. Pól a bhí ann. Bhí ionadh an domhain uirthi é a fheiceáil. 'Dia duit, a Phóil. Tar isteach,' arsa Máire.

'A Mháire, is ... is maith um ... bhuel ... is ... is ... is maith liom thu um ... is maith liom tusa agus an maith leat – bhuel – an maith leat ...'

Chuir Máire isteach air. 'Nóiméad amháin, a Phóil. Mise agus tusa!' arsa Máire. 'A Phóil, tá brón orm ach ní maith liom tusa ar an gcaoi sin. Is maith liom Seán agus ní maith liom aon bhuachaill eile. Agus tá Seán níos dathúla ná tusa. Tá brón orm a Phóil ach sin mar atá.'

'Tá brón orm. Maith dom é más é do thoil é ... Bhuel ... slán,' arsa Pól agus leis sin rith sé amach. Bhí náire an domhain air agus bhí sé gortaithe go mór.

An tráthnóna dar gcionn, tháinig Niamh ar cuairt chuig Máire.

'Dia duit, a Niamh. Tar isteach,' arsa Máire.

'Tá brón orm ach tá drochnuacht agam duit, a Mháire,' arsa Niamh. 'Ceapaim go bhfuil do bhuachaill Seán ag siúl amach le cailín eile mar chonaic mé é le Síle Ní Dhúill.'

'Á, níl an ceart agat, a Niamh,' arsa Máire. 'B'fhéidir gur bhuail sé léi ag an siopa.'

'Ach ... bh ...'.

'Bí ciúin anois. Ní aontaím leat! Tá sé i ngrá liomsa!' arsa Máire. 'Tá a fhios agam é. Tá muinín agam as.'

'Ceart go leor,' arsa Niamh. 'Ach bí cúramach!'

An lá ina dhiaidh sin nuair a bhuail Máire le Seán d'iarr sí air dul go dtí an phictiúrlann in éineacht léi an oíche sin.

'Tá brón orm ach beidh mé ag tabhairt aire do mo dheirfiúr anocht mar beidh mo thuismitheoirí ag dul amach,' ar seisean.

An lá dar gcionn bhí Máire ag dul le bronntanas a cheannach do lá breithe Niamh ach bhí Seán ag thabhairt cuairte ar a sheanmháthair a bhí san ospideál agus an lá ina dhiaidh sin bhí sé ag obair san ollmhargadh.

Ar an Mháirt chuir Máire glaoch teileafóin ar Sheán. 'A Sheáin, ar mhaith leat dul go dtí an phictiúrlann anocht?' arsa Máire.

'Níor mhaith,' arsa Seán, 'beidh mé ag imirt cluiche peile.'

'Cad mar gheall ar oíche amárach?' arsa Máire.

'B'fhéidir,' arsa Seán, 'ach níl a fhios agam anois. Cuirfidh mé glaoch ort amárach.'

D'fhan Máire sa teach i rith an lae ar fad ag feitheamh ar a ghlaoch teileafóin. Níor ghlaoigh sé ar a trí. Bhí díomá uirthi. Níor ghlaoigh sé ar a cúig ach oiread, ná ar a sé, ná ar a seacht. Bhí a fhios aici ansin go raibh rud éigin ar siúl.

Ar a naoi a chlog shocraigh Máire dul go teach Niamh chun a bronntanas a thabairt di. Bhí an doras ar oscailt agus chuaigh sí isteach.

'A Niamh, an bhfuil tú anseo? Tá bronntanas agam duit,' a deir sí.

Ansin chuala sí torann sa chistin. D'oscail sí an doras agus stop sí. Is beag nár thit sí i laige mar bhí Seán ann agus é ag tabhairt póige do Niamh.

Bhí croí Mháire ina béal aici.

Stop siad a luaithe is a chonaic siad í.

'A Mháire! Bhuel um – bhuel a Mháire,' arsa Niamh. 'Tá mé – bhuel – tá –'

'Bí ciúin!' arsa Máire. 'Tá tú an-ghlic. Tusa agus mo bhuachaillse lena chéile. Mo chara dílis an ea?' ar sise agus fearg uirthi. 'Agus tusa a Sheáin, mo stór! Bhí mé i ngrá leat agus …'

'Nílimid pósta, a Mháire' arsa Seán.

'Bí ciúin! Táim ag caint,' arsa Máire. 'Ní raibh tú ag an ollmhargadh, agus ní raibh tú ag tabhairt aire do Shineád, do dheirfiúr, bhí tú le Niamh, mo chara! Mo náire sibh. Tá sibh an-rúnda agus níl sibh dílis! Tá mé an-ghortaithe a Sheáin. Tá súil agam go mbeidh sibh sona sásta go deo,' ar sise agus leis sin rith sí as an teach agus í ag caoineadh.

Cúpla lá ina dhiaidh sin thosaigh sí ag smaoineamh ar Phól agus ar a chuid mothúchán seisean. Bhí aifeála uirthi faoi na rudaí a dúirt sí leis.

Ar an Aoine chonaic Máire Pól ag na siopaí agus chuaigh sí chun cainte leis. Bhí náire ar Phól nuair a chonaic sé í agus bhí sé an-chiúin. Thosaigh sé ag smaoineamh ar na rudaí a dúirt Máire leis agus ansin bhí dath dearg ar a aghaidh.

'Tá brón an domhain orm, a Phóil,' arsa Máire, 'mar ghortaigh mé thú leis na rudaí a dúirt mé leat. Is maith liom tusa, a Phóil, agus b'fhéidir gur mhaith leat dul ag scátáil liom tráthnóna éigin.'

'Ba mhaith liom é sin go mór, a Mháire,' arsa Pól. 'Glaofaidh mé ort ar an Satharn más mian leat.'

'Ceart go leor,' arsa Máire.

D'imigh siad ag scátáil ar an Satharn agus bhí an-spórt acu. Tharla an eachtra seo ar fad trí bliana ó shin, agus tá siad fós i ngrá lena chéile, agus an bheirt acu ag freastal ar an ollscoil.

B'fhéidir go bpósfaidís sa todhchaí. Agus cad faoi Niamh agus Seán? a déarfaidh tú. Bhuel sin scéal eile ach is fada an lá ó chonaic Máire nó Pól ceachtar acu.

BERNARD KEALY

The Pink Mini

Something pink catches eye.
Who'd dare to drive such a thing?
Ridiculous car.

Ruler

Ruler on the ground
Yellow stark upon the brown carpet,
It begs, 'Pick me up'.

A First Job

MARTIN HEHIR

This is a bright, candlelit room where the timers of lives are stored. Row upon row, shelf upon shelf of hourglasses. One for every person, each pouring the fine sand of lives being lived.

Now we see the owner of this room as he stalks about, examining the hourglasses. Now he picks up a plain, unadorned glass and stares an ice-cold stare. He sees a young man of around nineteen years of age, running down a street to the market. The owner of this room is The Grim Reaper, the Harvester of Souls, Death. He ponders for a few moments, and then he says, 'Yes ... He'll do'.

Jason Mahon ran down the street, his father and John O'Grady, a neighbour, sitting by the wall, were talking and watching him.

John: 'Well, Jim ... Jason is nearly nineteen. He's gonna have to get a job soon.'

Moment's thought.

John: 'Look, Jim. I've got nuttin' against 'em. He's a real nice lad an' all dat, it's just ... You know ... the trouble with him is ...'

Jim: 'I know, he couldn't find his behind using both his hands.'

Moment's thought again.

John: 'Hey, why don't yah take 'em down to de local job market this afternoon. Yah never know ... you might stick 'em up doin' something.'

Jim: 'O.K. I'll do that. Thanks.'

It is 11.30 a.m. on the 24th of August 1749. In Cork town there are lots of young men with their fathers at the square.

'Well, what do you think you'd like to be, son?' Jim asked Jason.

'I think I'd like to be a carpenter,' said Jason.

'The job market starts in half-an-hour, so let's get you a new suit of clothes,' his dad said.

Fifteen minutes later, Jim emerged from a tailor's shop with Jason, who was wearing a very odd suit of clothes.

'That's a very nice suit you're wearing, son,' commented Jim.

'I hope so!' said Jason.

'No, really, Jas, it is a very good fit.'

'It will be a good fit if I grow up to be an eighteen-legged elephant!' joked Jason.

'No, come on, Jas. There are thousands of young lads who would be very grateful to have a warm garment like that.'

'Could I share it with them?' asked Jason hopefully.

It was a quarter to twelve that night, and Jason was the only one left in the market. 'Come on, son,' said Jim to Jason, 'we'd better be headin' 'ome.'

'The market doesn't close 'till twelve!' declared Jason, still a tinge of hope in his voice.

'All right, we'll wait another while,' his father consented.

The chat was interrupted by the clip-clop of the hooves of a horse as it slowed up. There was a chilling silence as the robed, hooded rider dismounted. The atmosphere was spoiled when the robed figure slipped and fell.

'Oh, bugger!' uttered the robed figure.

Jason ran over to help him up, and was surprised to find the robed figure had hands of bone.

'Thank you,' said the figure, his face completely shrouded in the folds of his hood. 'What you see and hear will not be what your father sees and hears,' the figure told him.

'Do you want to make my son an apprentice?' asked Jim optimistically.

'Yes,' answered the figure, 'I do.'

'Well, what do you do?' asked Jim.

'I deliver souls to Heaven and Hell,' replied the figure.

'It sounds very important,' commented Jim.

'It is,' said the figure.

'Well, Jason, do you want the job?' questioned Jim.

'I think I'll take it,' responded Jason.

At this the robed figure put Jason on the back of his horse.

'Pardon me, sir, but are you Death?' asked Jason.

'Correct! Full marks for observation,' answered Death. 'First of all, we'll get you a new suit of clothes.'

'These are new today – yesterday, I mean.'

'Really?'

'Father said the shop was famous for its budget clothing,' remarked Jason.

'Well that certainly adds a new terror to poverty,' quipped Death.

Jason was very surprised at how fast the horse galloped, and screamed when it left the ground.

'Don't worry,' assured Death. 'It takes a little getting used to,' he added. The horse soon landed in Dublin.

'Why isn't your horse just bones?' asked Jason.

'I used to have one of them, but it is a pain having to get off and stick the bones back on all the time,' answered Death.

Soon the two of them came out of a clothes shop, Jason wearing clothes of the latest fashion.

'I don't understand why these shops are open all night,' commented Jason.

'A Dublin merchant can't sleep thinking about the money he's not making,' replied Death. 'Well, we have had enough fun for one night, let's get back to business,' said Death. And with that they both got on the horse and Death took out an hourglass. 'Not much time left,' he said. He flicked his heels and the horse set off at a trot, then a canter, and then a gallop. The wind roared in Jason's ears as the horse left the ground and soon they touched down behind a country cabin.

Death pulled the hourglass from his robes, and then pulled a scythe out of its holder. He said, 'Come on, Jason. Follow me and watch. You may be asked questions later.' They both went into the cabin and saw a man who looked at least fifty. Death brought the scythe around in a double-handed swing that passed through the man. The man's spirit walked out of its body and flew off.

'Is it always like that?' Jason asked.

'Yes, but you use a sword for noble people. It's traditional,' Death answered.

Death gave Jason a few more lessons over the next few days. Jason found life in Death's residence very comfortable. Death had a manservant called Albert. Albert was a very jittery old man who made all the food. Soon Jason began to question the reason for getting this job. Finally he went up to Death and asked him why.

'You may as well be told now,' Death sighed. 'I'm thinking of retiring.'

'Retiring?' Jason repeated, shocked.

'For a while anyway,' Death said. 'Don't worry. You'll get the hang of the job soon. I thought I would try being a human. You know, get a job, go fishing, that sort of thing,' Death added.

'Yeah, well, does that mean that I have to go and do all the work? I mean, what happens if I have problems?' Jason inquired.

'You won't,' Death assured him.

Death said goodbye and left. Soon he was entering a very unusual pub. He made his way to the counter. 'What is that green one?' Death asked after an hour. The landlord peered at the label.

'It says it's Melon Brandy,' he said doubtfully. 'It says it's bottled by some monks to an ancient recipe,' he added.

'I will try it,' Death said.

The man looked sideways at the empty glasses on the counter.

'Are you sure you haven't had enough?' he asked.

It worried him vaguely that he couldn't seem to make out the stranger's face. The glass disappeared into the hood and came out empty.

'No. I don't see the point,' Death commented.

'Sorry?' the landlord asked.

'What is supposed to happen?'

'How many drinks have you had?'

'Forty-seven.'

'Just about anything, at that stage,' said the barman, thinking it was closing time. 'I'm sorry, but it's a quarter-to-three,' he said.

'I get the message,' Death said, getting up and heading for the door. Failure. But what about a job?

'And what was your previous position?'

'I ushered souls into the next world.'

'Yes, but do you have any particular skills?'

Death thought about it. 'I suppose a certain amount of expertise with agricultural implements,' he ventured.

The young man shook his firmly.

'No?'

'This is a city, Mr Death. I would have thought you would have prepared for something more refined than working with agricultural implements. Have you ever thought of going into teaching?' the man asked.

Death's face was a mask of terror. Well, it was always a mask of terror, but this time he meant it to be. He had had enough.

'Look,' he said lifting up his hood.

The man nearly fainted.

'Settle down,' Death said. 'You've got a good few years left.'

'It's true!' the man exclaimed. 'I thought you were a nightmare!'

'I could take offence at that,' Death said.

'You really are Death? Well, let's see, um, er, well, I've got a job as a cook ...'

'I'll take it.'

After about a week, Death had settled in his job. He had bought a cat, and he had it in the kitchen with him. The owner of the foodshop was delighted with his work. He was responsible for the number of customers that was getting very high. Business was booming. That evening, the owner was closing up when Death came over.

'Do you always have this many customers?' he asked.

'No, er, yes,' the owner answered.

'I see. Thanks again for the job.'

'Think nothing of it. By the way, how come your voice goes to my brain without going in my ears?'

'What?'

'Er, nothing.'

'Good. Well, I'll be off. Goodbye.'

That night there was a terrible fire at the foodshop. When Death heard, he was extremely unhappy.

'I'll try once more,' he said.

He applied for a docker's job in the port. When the man in charge saw how weak he looked, he said, 'Look, April Fool's Day is next year, chum. Get lost!'

Death had finally had enough. He walked to a hidden corner and emitted a very high-pitched whistle. His horse heard it instantly, and galloped out, much to Jason's surprise. When it returned, a very unhappy looking Death was riding it.

'I'm back,' he said.

Jason: 'What happened?'

Death: 'You name it.'

Jason: 'Bad?'

Death: 'Very.'

Jason: 'I take it you want your job back, then.'

Death: 'Very accurate.'

Jason: 'Goodbye, then ... it's such an unpleasant word, isn't it?'

Death: 'Quite so! (grinning) Prefer *slán leat*.'

Thus ended Jason Mahon's first job.

Contributors

ABC by Vicky Dillon. Vicky is 10 years old, comes from Terenure, Dublin, and goes to Presentation Primary School, Terenure.

The Hungry Vacuum Cleaner by Niamh ní Ghallchóir. Niamh is 10 years old, comes from Glasnevin, Dublin, and attends Scoil Mobhi, Glasnevin.

The Spider by Deirdre ní Mhuirthile. Deirdre is 12 years old and comes from Glaunthaune, Co. Cork. She goes to Coláiste an Phiarsaigh, Gleann Maghair.

Milltowncross by Stephen Bennett. Stephen is 10 years old and comes from Tyrrellspass, Co. Westmeath. He goes to Tyrrellspass National School.

War by Michael Ross. Michael is 11 years old and lives near Mallow, Co. Cork. He goes to Adare National School, Fermoy.

An Taibhse by Tomás Ó Spealláin. Tomás is 12 years old and lives in Ennis, Co. Clare. He goes to Gaelscoil Mhíchíl Cíosóg, Inis.

M.E. and Me by Kathy Clifford. Kathy is 12 years old and lives in Galway city. She goes to Scoil Raois, Taylor's Hill.

Eating an Apple by Graham Mullane. Graham is 7 years old and lives in Gurranabraher, Cork. He attends Churchfield National School, Cork.

An Páistín by Séamus de Nais. Séamus is 9 years old and lives in Caisleán Nua Thiar, Co. Luimnigh. He attends Gaelscoil O Doghair, Co Luimnigh.

The Robber by Suzanne Rath. Suzanne is 7 years old and lives in Gorey, Co. Wexford. She attends Kilnamanagh National School, Co. Wexford.

Rary by Doireann ní Ghríofa. Doireann is 10 years old and lives in Ennis, Co. Clare. She attends Gaelscoil Mhíchíl Cíosóg, Inis.

When I Grow Up by Sarah Aherne. Sarah is 9 years old and lives in Athlone, Co. Roscommon. She attends Ballybay National School, Athlone.

Mo Pheann Draíochta by Séamus de Nais. See **An Páistín** (above).

The Ballad of Mary Whyte by Eimear Lynch. Eimear is 13 years old and lives in Killiney, Co. Dublin. She attends St Joseph of Cluny School, Killiney.

An Taibhse by Dylan Ó Searcaí. Dylan is 11 years old and lives in Raheny, Dublin. He attends Belvedere Boys School, Clontarf.

Dew in a Cobweb and Snow by Daire Mac Raois. Daire is 12 years old and lives in Bray, Co. Wicklow. He has just moved from Scoil Chulainn, Bray, to secondary school at Coláiste Eoin, Dublin.

The Lonely Fox by Emily Egan. Emily is 10 years old and lives in Athlone, Co. Westmeath. She attends Coosan National School, Athlone.

An Guthán by Bríd de Faoite. Bríd is 13 years old and lives in An Rinn, Co. Portláirge. She attends Scoil San Nioclás, An Rinn.

Beidh Mé Ann by Hilda Flynn. Hilda is 14 years old, lives in Ardfinnan, Co. Tipperary, and attends Presentation Secondary School, Clonmel.

The Exodus from Ireland by Michael O'Sullivan. Michael is 12 years old and lives in Wilton, Cork. He attends Coláiste an Spioraid Naoimh, Bishopstown, Cork.

The Day the Dust Blew In by Layla O'Mara. Layla is 12 years old, lives in Delgany, Co. Wicklow, and attends the Bray School Project.

Oil by Saba Rahmani. Saba is 14 years old, lives in Glanmire, Co. Cork and attends Christian Brothers College, Sydney Hill, Cork.

Last Christmas by Sarah Ryan. Sarah is 14 years old, lives in Pallasgreen, Co. Limerick, and attends the Convent of Mercy, Doon, Co. Limerick.

My Doggie by Emma Long. Emma is 6 years old, lives in Bishopstown, Cork, and attends Scoil an Spioraid Naoimh, Bishopstown.

My Home by Cliodhna Martin. Cliodhna is 9 years old, lives in Sandycove, Co. Dublin, and attends Loreto Abbey Primary School, Dalkey.

James's Quest by Seamus O'Brien. Seamus is 12 years old, lives in Portlaoise, Co. Laois and attends CBS National School, Portlaoise.

Life on a Farm by Anna-Marie Higgins. Anna-Marie is 8 years old and lives in Mountbellew, Co. Galway. She attends Moylougha National School, Mountbellew.

A Shark Called Bugsy Brown by Alison McClelland. Alison is 5½ years old, lives in Tallaght, Dublin, and attends Presentation Primary School, Terenure, Dublin.

Trees in Winter by Rahmona Henry. Rahmona is 10 years old, lives in Johnstown, Co. Roscommon, and attends Cornafulla National School, Athlone, Co. Roscommon.

Trees by Miriam Sweeney. Miriam is 6 years old, lives in Rathfarnham, Dublin, and attends Loreto National School, The Grange, Rathfarnham.

The Quest of the Sarakai by Mark Fottrell. Mark is 14 years old, lives in Leixlip, Co. Kildare, and attends Coláiste Chiaráin, Celbridge, Co. Kildare.

An Tuaisceart by Niall mac Innéirí. Niall is 12 years old, lives in Caisleán Nua Thiar, Co. Luimnigh, and attends Gaelscoil O Doghair, Co. Luimnigh.

Don't Worry, Be Yourself by Ruth Finneran. Ruth is 14 years old, lives in Navan, Co. Meath. She attends St. Michael's Loreto Convent, Navan.

The Friendly Giant by Emer Delaney. Emer is 6 years old, lives in Blackrock, Co. Dublin, and goes to Muckross Park Junior School, Donnybrook, Dublin.

Avenging the Grape by Geraldine Hayes. Geraldine is 13 years old, lives in Ballygall, Dublin, and attends St. Mary's H.F.C., Glasnevin, Dublin.

Am Taistil by Dara de Búrca. Dara is 11 years old, lives in Ceatharlach and attends Gaelscoil Eoghain Uí Thuairisc, Ceatharlach.

The Crab and **The Duck** by Gillian McCusker. Gillian is 11 years old, lives in Delgany, Co. Wicklow, and attends St. Brigid's School, Greystones, Co. Wicklow.

The Snail by Isobel Abbott. Isobel lives in Mullingar, Co. Westmeath, and attends Loreto College, Mullingar.

Saol Mogwa by Miriam nic Artúir. Miriam is 11 years old and attends Gaelscoil Mhíchíl Cíosóg, Inis, Co. an Chláir.

Rain by Peter Killian. Peter is 9 years old, lives in near Athlone, Co. Roscommon, and attends Cornafulla National School, Athlone.

The Tale of a Goblin by Ruth MacNamara. Ruth is 14 years old, lives in Dundalk, Co. Louth, and attends Dundalk Grammar School.

Oceania, Flower of the Deep by Una Harnett. Una is 13 years old, and attends Rosemont Park School, Blackrock, Co. Dublin.

Peig Sayers by Kathleen Treacy. Kathleen is 15 years old and attends the Convent of Mercy, Doon, Co. Limerick.

My Brother and **The Ship** by Alice Hamilton. Alice is 7 years old, lives in Skerries, Co. Dublin, and attends Holmpatrick National School, Skerries.

A Gruesome Discovery by Peter Durkan. Peter is 12 years old, lives in Castlebar, Co. Mayo, and attends St. Patrick's National School, Castlebar.

An Cúl by Aoife ní Ghliasáin. Aoife is 14 years old, lives in Portmarnock, Co. Dublin, and attends St Mary's Secondary School, Baldoyle.

I Believe by Neal Brophy. Neal is 9 years old, lives in Sandymount, Dublin, and attends R.M.D.S., Ranelagh, Dublin.

An Dara Seans by Aoife ní Ghliasáin. See **An Cúl** (above).

The Pink Mini and **Ruler** by Bernard Kealy. Bernard is 13 years old, lives near Tralee, Co. Kerry, and attends St Mary's Secondary School, Tralee.

A First Job by Martin Hehir. Martin is 11 years old and attends Kinsealy National School, Co. Dublin.

Attention!
YOUNG WRITERS

Over 5,000 entries
were judged for possible
inclusion in this book.

❧ ❧ ❧

Don't be left out of the next
book to be published in 1994.

❧ ❧ ❧

Look out for details of the
competition when you return to
school after the summer
holidays.

❧ ❧ ❧

Ask your English teacher or
principal or call into your local
McDonald's restaurant
for details.

OTHER BOOKS FROM THE O'BRIEN PRESS

Off We Go . . . 1
THE DUBLIN ADVENTURE
Siobhán Parkinson
Illustrated by Cathy Henderson
Dara and his big sister Sinéad are in Dublin for the first time. City life is new to them, with all its strange ways.
A witty and informative account of a first visit to Dublin.

Off We Go . . . 2
THE COUNTRY ADVENTURE
Siobhán Parkinson
Illustrated by Cathy Henderson
Michelle lives in Dublin and knows a thing or two. She knows that country people are a bit peculiar. But when she visits Sinéad and Dara, her country cousins, she discovers she has a lot to learn.
A funny and revealing look at life on a farm through the eyes of a young city-slicker.

THE LEPRECHAUN WHO WISHED HE WASN'T
Siobhán Parkinson
Laurence is a leprechaun who has been small for 1100 years and is sick of it! He wants to be TALL. He wants to be cool. Then he meets Phoebe, a large girl who wants to be small.
A tall tale indeed.

Dingwell Street School Stories
THE FISHFACE FEUD
Martin Waddell
Illustrated by Arthur Robins
The honour of class P6 is at stake when Ernie Flack and friends take on Fishface Duggan and his gang from P7 in this lively story.

RUBBERNECK'S REVENGE
Martin Waddell
Illustrated by Arthur Robins
Ernie Flack and his friends find themselves in Heap Big Trouble when the Deputy Head goes on the warpath in this action-packed Dingwell Street School story.

THE SCHOOL THAT WENT TO SEA
Martin Waddell
Illustrated in full colour by Leo Hartas
Imagine if it rained so hard your school floated away, like a ship, out to sea. That is what happens in this story – and everyone is very pleased that they have a clever teacher like Ms Smith on board to guide them.

LITTLE STAR
Marita Conlon-McKenna
Illustrated in full colour by Christopher Coady
A first picture book from Ireland's favourite author.
A story for little ones – a tale of intimacy, feeling and charm.

WHIZZ QUIZ
Seán O'Leary
Illustrated by Ann O'Leary
Chockful of quizzes and fantastic puzzles on every topic under the sun. Great fun – and educational too!

THAT PEST JONATHAN
William Cole
Illustrated by Tomi Ungerer
The thing that Jonathan liked best was being a pest! Or so it seemed to his parents, so they took him to see Doctor Carrother. But his answer to their little problem is unexpected.

BOOKS FOR OLDER CHILDREN

UNDER THE HAWTHORN TREE
Marita Conlon-McKenna
Eily, Michael and Peggy find themselves alone during the Great Famine in Ireland in the 1840s. They set off on a long journey to try to find their great-aunts. *A classic story.*

WILDFLOWER GIRL
Marita Conlon-McKenna
Peggy, from *Under the Hawthorn Tree,* is now thirteen and must leave Ireland for America. After a terrible journey on board ship, she arrives in Boston. What kind of life will she find there?

THE BLUE HORSE
Marita Conlon-McKenna
When their caravan burns down, Katie's family must move to live in a house in a new estate. But for Katie, this means trouble. Is she strong enough to deal with the new situation?

THE TAIN
Liam MacUistin
The great classic Celtic tale, full of the excitement of the battle, and ending with the terrible fight to the death between best friends Cuchulainn and Ferdia.

STRONGBOW
Morgan Llywelyn
The dramatic story of the Norman conquest of Ireland in the twelfth century, as told by Strongbow and by Aoife Mac Murrough, the Irish princess whom he married.

BRIAN BORU
Morgan Llywelyn
The exciting story of High King Brian Boru and of tenth-century Ireland brought vividly to life as never before.

THE CASTLE IN THE ATTIC
Elizabeth Winthrop
There is a strange legend attached to the model castle given to William by Mrs Phillips. He is drawn into the story when the silver knight who guards the castle comes to life.

BIKE HUNT
Hugh Galt

Niall Quinn's new bike is stolen and he is determined to find it. Helped by the skill of Katie, and by his friend Paudge, Niall becomes entangled in a dangerous situation in the Wicklow Mountains.

HORSE THIEF
Hugh Galt

Rory's beloved old mare disappears. Then three girls discover a racehorse kidnapped and being held for ransom near their home. These two stories interweave into a nail-biting story, full of action and thrills.

Other World Series 1

OCTOBER MOON
Michael Scott

Rachel Stone and her family move into Seasonstown House, and then the trouble begins. Who or what wants to get rid of them? *A scary story, with a chilling ending.*

Other World Series 2

GEMINI GAME
Michael Scott

When Liz and BJ O'Connor discover that the computer game they have made develops a virus, they must travel into the Virtual Reality world to solve the problem. But there they find dangers they have never before seen. Can they make it back to normal life again?

THE DRUID'S TUNE
Orla Melling
Two teenage visitors to Ireland are hurled into the ancient past and become involved in the life of Cuchulainn and in the fearsome battle of the Táin.

Send for our full colour catalogue to:

THE O'BRIEN PRESS
20 Victoria Road, Dublin 6, Ireland